Climbing Mountai

The Alps, Pyrenees and bits bet

By Andrew Leckenby

For those at the bridge

Whiskey Woo - Adopted ex PDSA
Tetley 'Tets' - Adopted ex RSPCA
Dino 'Dog'- Adoted ex TIA
Hank 'The Hank Man'- Fostered ex Bristol Dawg

For those by the fire

Blue 'Bluesy'- Adoptee ex RSPCA
Maggie 'three toes' Moo - Adoptee ex RGT East Riding
Lucy 'underfoot' loo - Foster ex RGT East Riding
Frank 'The Lump' Frankles - Foster ex RGT East Riding

Foreword

Every year countless thousands of Greyhounds and other sight hounds are bred for racing and working. Every year the same number are abandoned, ill-treated and destroyed when they fail to make the grade,

The lucky ones find their way into a rescue kennel, the really lucky ones find that the kennel is heated with a comfy bed, only too few make it to their very own forever sofa, finally in the care of a human that wants no more than the unconditional love these animals have to offer.

Many of these scared abandoned hounds find themselves in a council pound, literally unwanted and unloved, for no reason other than they could no longer run fast enough.

Due to the massive numbers of dogs of all varieties finding their fate in a council pound they are only given 7 days. Unlike left luggage there is no auction or charity give away, these poor hounds are simply destroyed and cast onto the funeral pyre.

There is a glimmer of hope, around the country countless volunteers run rescues, foster and adopt, a common theme amongst hound owners is one is never enough.

The hounds on death row can be found a comfy rescue and hopefully onto a sofa **BUT** a hound finding itself in a council pound cannot move straight into a rescue kennel due to the possibility of it having contracted a communicable disease, so these hounds need a period of isolation kenneling and this is an expense many small rescues cannot meet on a regular basis.

Sight hounds Online was an online community that became a charity to spread awareness and raise funds to help all sight hounds in need regardless of where they are. Their last drive was to create a fund primarily to provide for emergency isolation kenneling for hounds in council pounds that have a rescue place waiting but no means to get them there.

Mountains for Mutts is the story of my attempt to raise money for the SOL emergency kennel fund.

On behalf of me and the mutts I would like to take this opportunity to thank you dear reader, for purchasing this book, every copy sold includes a donation to a greyhound charity. If you have borrowed, stolen or otherwise come across this book and find yourself enjoying it please consider making a small donation to your local hound pound.

Thanks and Enjoy

Andrew

Prologue

Call me an old romantic but there is something special about the Alps.

Who hasn't watched the Italian job or Goldfinger and wanted to drive a sports car on winding snow lined ribbons of asphalt, wearing shades listening to Matt Monroe?

Who hasn't read the Cannon and wanted to climb the fabled Reichenbach falls to see where Holmes finally rid the world of the evil that was Moriaty?

Who wouldn't want to walk on a Glacier? Follow the footsteps of Hannibal? Drive a road called the Furka pass? Sit by a lake of glorious cobalt blue higher than planes fly?

It all started seven years ago I suppose. An internet forum organised a week long road trip to Prague. I had never driven abroad and opted to travel as a passenger sharing fuel costs. A real boys own adventure, despite being nearly forty at the time, and of the 50 or so participants, many of them couples, I was far from the oldest.

It was a roller coaster of a week, from 150 mph on a German Autobahn, driving through an historic monument in the center of Prague, being nearly arrested for racing on an abandoned cold war runway in deepest Czechoslovakia, and how many people will have done a respectably fast lap of the Nurburgring in strangers car with a boot full of duty free and that had to get three of us to Dunkirk the same night?

Loved it so much I was home for all of 2 nights before a ferry had been booked for the following weekend and swmbo (she who must be obeyed) was being whisked off to France for 3 days driving down to Millau and back via the Nurburgring. This continental driving lark is fun.

Back in blighty and someone on the forum had come up with the bright idea of a completely European road trip, a week searching out the best driving roads in Europe (yes Briskoda did beat Top Gear!) lots of ideas where bandied about, The Stelvio pass, the Col du Turini, the Bernard passes, but as time passed the OP (original poster) didn't want the hassle of the organisation and the idea was in danger of faltering.

See above, this was happening even if I had to do it all myself! Sticking pins in a map for all the roads that had been mentioned it was just a case of joining the dots with the squiggliest route possible.

The fact that the route started to pass through such glorious places as Nice and Monaco was pure good luck. Nine of us set out on that trip and a book will be written of our exploits. It led to a further epic of a journey over 3 weeks taking in 11 countries and a swan song a year later of a shorter tour but in much more powerful machinery.

Several things came out of these journeys,

I don't speak French, Italian, German, or Czech but can get by after a few days of listening.

I like foreign food.

Driving over 1000 miles in 24 hours is hard work.

Driving 100 miles + in the Alps in a day is hard work

Driving in the Alps requires immense concentration

Sat Nav is crap.

I had a natural talent for route making.

Motorcyclists are complete nutters, remove all enjoyment from driving and have a death wish that unfortunately seems to be all too frequently answered.

Cyclists are even nuttier than motorcyclists, appearing anywhere with the hint of a slope, uphill impossible to get round, downhill too fast in the corners, too slow in the straights.

On our trips we used walkie talkies when travelling in convoy, the lead car giving the all clear on the overtakes, all that could be heard over the airwaves would be clear, clear, clear, BLOODY CYCLISTS!!

JUNE 2011

The family were holidaying once again in Wales at a small farm that hires out cottages and a caravan, each one set in its own paddock where the hounds can have free rein. (Little Dumpledale) There is also a hot tub and swimming pool for the humans.

Looking down all I could see was my overly large belly, not a pretty sight for the rest of the farms guests, in fact quite embarrassing. Somehow I had let my weight bloom up to 110kg. Don't get me wrong I wasn't lazy or unfit, being a posty kept me relatively fit, but I did enjoy my food and snacking was certainly taking its toll.

Thinking things over I wondered what I could do to turn the tide. A few years earlier I had successfully shed a few pounds cycling and my trusty Ridgeback Delta, an overweight hybrid itself and heading towards its 15th year. Strolling round a local supermarket I picked up a couple of cycling mags and began to peruse the pages.

Never one to do anything by halves I decided that a racing bike with mm wide tyres really wasn't going to stand up to my weight and yet another hybrid didn't float my boat, I wanted sleek and sexy, a professional bike but without the perceived discomfort.

As I mentioned not doing things by halves I started looking at drop barred tourers, and if a touring bike then I wanted the best, reading the mags and various online reviews the Ridgeback Panorama world tour stood out. My previous Ridgeback had weathered 15 years of suffering and here was a bike from the same manufacturer, made from steel and advertised as being able to tour the world. Certainly coming equipped with all the racks, bottle cages, pumps etc that anyone could wish for it looked the part and, to my mind, told the world the rider was a seasoned cyclist who knew what he was doing.

Kerching £1400 lighter I had my new bike.

July 2011

After riding the new bike for a few miles and having had the
warning from swmbo that after spending a months wages I had
better ride the bloody thing I started looking at equipment, wow how
easy is it to spend money? Padded shorts, the odd cycling jersey,
new pedals ....

August 2011

Having managed to complete around 40 miles in one sitting I was quite proud of my cycling achievements. Scanning the internet looking to see how my progress was, well progressing, I came across a fantastic cycling forum, 'cyclechat.net' On cyclechat I read of other peoples exploits and touring ambitions, from cycling Lands End to John O Groats to cycling the world.

I should at this point mention that at home we entertained three gorgeous greyhounds, two we had adopted from various places and a poor old chappy who suffered from arthritis, corns, and general malaise. Hank was our foster hound having arrived from Romford via Bristol he was now residing in Bradford. How he came to be under my roof was a convoluted story but was basically down to a web based charity SOL for whom I also did some moderating.

Combining the two I came up with a great money raising idea, I would cycle around the country and each night a SOL supporter could give me a bed for the night and all the money I raised could go towards looking after ill abandoned and abused hounds, sorted, not only would the dogs profit, I would get fit and the outlay on the bike would be completely justified, even to the notorious swmbo!!

More money was quickly disposed of in the purchasing of a cycling specific sat-nav, after all I would need to find my way around, wouldn't I?

Nearing the end of August I came across a posting on cyclechat asking if anyone fancied a forum ride, one of the members regularly organized a ride out starting in nearby Hebden Bridge.

Never one to bite of two much I signed up and set off, firstly riding the 15 miles or so to the start point and then setting off into the hills on what turned out to be a 100 km circular route. Not having any choice but to get home I cycled the full distance getting off and pushing on just one hill!! Thank goodness I had purchased a touring bike with comfy wide tyres (32mm) and a touring crank set (Triple 28/ 32 being the easiest gear).

September 2011

One step forwards, two steps back.

One thing I had noticed is that most riders rode clipless, being attached to the bike and enabling more power to be applied to the pedaling action, not least of all because it allows force to be applied on the up stroke as well as the down. I really didn't fancy this malarkey so purchased some plastic toecaps that would allow my foot to be held in position like old fashioned toe clips but without the straps and risk of getting caught up.

My new cyclechat buddy (Colin) was organizing another ride from Hebden, so being a glutton for punishment I signed up. I had made some improvements to the bike and was looking forward to having another crack at a century ride, hopefully without pushing!!

I made it nearly to Halifax, about halfway to Hebden Bridge before practically bursting into tears at the pain that was shooting through my right knee. Four years earlier I had fractured my tibial plateau and my knee area still contains a rod a couple of plates and a few pins, I thought this was the end of my cycling career before it had started.

The planned tour was all to pot as well, despite SOL having many 'friends' and members their locations of those willing to accommodate a stranger for the night where spread rather far and wide, the whole fundraising thing needed a serious rethink even if I could cycle more than 5 miles in the future!!

Turning once again to the internet and 'cyclechat' I started to read about bike fit and knee problems, it appeared that the pain I had experienced was quite common for people riding clipless pedals whose cleats where set in the wrong position, forcing their knees to move through an unnatural plane. Due to my metalwork I did have a slight bow and on examination saw that my knee did not follow a straight up and down motion when pedaling. In order to achieve this I found that I needed to point my toes outward at about 12°

something that the plastic toecaps would not allow.

After some experimentation, offsetting one of the toeclips on the pedal meant my knee appeared to follow the correct direction!

October 2011

Colin had posted about a ride that occurred annually from Hebden Bridge called an audax. Unlike a sportive, an audax has no signposts only a route card and there are no feed stations or mechanical back up, an audax can be any length from 50km up to 1400km and the distance as to be completed with a specific time frame. Something that appealed to me about audaxing, being a tight wad, was the price, unlike sportives audaxes usually cost under a tenner!

The Audax Colin spoke of was the Season of Mists and is 100km long with approximately 2,500m of climbing.

Armed with my modified pedals I turned up at the start point, expecting (from what I had read) a load of bearded blokes on old steel bikes, or at least touring bikes like my own. Err no, carbon fiber race bikes where very much the order of the day, not another pannier rack could be seen, let alone a top box full of 'survival' kit. Certainly front racks were overkill and the 3 water bottles that adorned my frame did lead to some comments, but at least I wasn't going thirsty!

Steady away, I was quicker than some, which gave me great encouragement, and slower than others (no surprise) and I did have to stop on one hill, which is where my problems started my modified toe holder kept working its way loose and rotating which meant setting off on any hill of any sort was dangerous at best. Fortunately a fellow cyclist stopped and helped in the tightening process, (two spanners are better than one) but it was short lived, either superglue was needed or a rethink.

There had to be a solution, I couldn't be the only rider with wonky knee, clipless appeared to be out of the question as this kept your foot rigid, I needed freedom of movement whilst still wanting to be attached to the pedal. FROGS, a company called Speedplay make a type of pedal for the Mtb rider that have complete free float whilst till securing the rider to the pedal and offering an easy unclip. Ordered!

November 2011

The new pedals had arrived and were a revelation, on the monthly forum rides of 100 Miles!! Gone was the knee ache, in was the ability to add that extra power on the uphills and no more bouncing off the pedal with abrupt or missed gear changes. Of course the downside was the scuffed and bruised hip from my first clipless moment when at the café stop the guy in front stopped slightly abruptly and I forgot to twist my foot free from the
pedal before coming to a halt and toppling unceremoniously sideways.

The tour of Britain was well and truly in the doldrums, not only was accommodation scarce in forth coming, in all honesty I wasn't particularly enthusiastic about riding for days on our road system. From what I had witnessed on my various outings the road surface was crap, the tolerance of road users was zero, and the rain was the only guaranteed companion.

Something had to be thought of, once more scouring the net I read a blog of some young lady who had started out in a similar position to myself (though she was half my age) and had completed a ride from London to Paris for charity. That sounded more like it, a mini bus to carry all the gear, an hotel every night with prepared meals and a lift home at the end!! Sign me up and get son interested, he can come as well.

Downside, well yes you could specify your own charity, but you had to pay the organizing company nearly £1000 for the privilege of cycling for 4 days, hang about, it didn't cost me that to do a 3 week road trip let alone cycle for 3 days through France.

Hmm a 3 week road trip, I had done this before, through the most spectacular scenery on the planet, and all the while I had seen BLOODY CYCLISTS. If other folk could do it then why couldn't I? How hard could it be, pass me a map.

Coming down to earth I started to think about the logistics of touring on the continent. Living in Bradford it is a 300 mile journey to

Dover and that is on the motorway, of my 3 weeks holiday potentially 12 days would be spent travelling to the ferry and back on roads that quite frankly I didn't want to cycle on. In any case with all the equipment required for 3 weeks touring would 50 miles in a day be feasible? That's 85km which I knew I could cycle as a one off, maybe even every weekend, but every day? This cycle fitness thing and stamina really needed looking into.

Ok so you are getting bored of reading it but again the internet and 'cyclechat' was the answer. Reading members travelogues and blog postings the consensus of opinion was that so long as you could cycle 100k in a day then 70k on a loaded tourer was doable and on tours people tend to tour themselves fit rather than go all out and peak beforehand.

The best find though was the bike bus, a bus and trailer that picks passengers / luggage and bikes up at points the length of Britain and deposits them at points the length of France alternating between Eastern and Western France weekly. Back to that map!

December 2011

So far the weight as been falling off, from a size 40" to a 36" waist, costly but worth it, luckily the cycling gear I had bought was a tad tight to start with, now it all fits perfect.

The map has proved very useful I have managed to devise a route across France that will take in many of the iconic climbs that the tour de France uses, some I had already driven previously and in a perverse way I thought this will give me Kudos in the cycling fraternity.

Cycling in the area I had with hills that regularly hit gradients of 14% in my naive way I thought how hard can an Alp be where the gradient is pretty much pegged at <10%?

So the route, a tad over 1000 miles, the various planning applications I had used for my sat nav suggested an overall height gain of 26,000m + no problems!!

The first day was to be around 80km and had a height gain of approximately 2100m, posting this on cyclechat for opinions for a touring route with regard to length and height to see if I was in the ball park with seasoned tourers led to interesting responses. In general was deemed doable but not really suitable on the first day of a first tour on a fully laden bike. I have mentioned I don't do things by halves haven't I? Besides for the trip to work it would be necessary.

Next job was to get support and charitable donations, posting my plans on every cycling and hound website I could find the money soon started coming in to my donation page, at this point I realized I had made it impossible to pull out, I really would have to go through with this.

That night the cold shivers started. I spoke schoolboy French at best, I hadn't been on holiday or abroad completely on my own ever. Oh and my sense of direction is none existent.. Add into the mix that I was the wrong side of 40, been cycling only six months, and here I was planning on cycling the same roads the Tour de France professionals struggle on, yet I would be doing it on a loaded touring bike. GULP.

Whilst fitness might come from touring, I quickly realized it would be good idea to experience long climbs before actually setting off and that my fitness wasn't being helped by the bike sitting in the shed due to the lousy weather.

Sweet talking swmbo into (another) Christmas present I managed to find a 2010 Giant Defy road bike in the sales and searching for an indoor trainer on which to use it discovered the TACX genius. OK so it cost an arm and a leg, and would need a new computer system to run it, but I could buy videos for it or even input my own routes and it would faithfully follow them on google maps. The glory of this system is it allows you to alter the resistance depending on the riders' weight and automatically adjusts for terrain changes up to about 15%. In theory this meant I could cycle my entire route in the comfort of my bedroom whilst experiencing the hardships of a loaded touring bike! So swmbo agreed and the TACX was installed. Oh my god what have I let myself in for, I managed to install all the software and my day 1 route, in three parts. The first part, 30km or so that was probably the flattest part of the day nearly killed me, even with a gigantic fan blowing cold air at me the sweat was pouring from every pore. I was seriously unfit, this was going to have to be my daily regime for some time to come.

The Route

Let me introduce you to my proposed route, the aforementioned Bicycle express had a drop of point in Valence in the East and 3 weeks later a pick up point in Lourdes to the West. Between these two points lies just about whatever terrain you would like to traverse.

Being a glutton for punishment, wanting to raise as much money as possible, and being selfish and wanting bragging rights a straight line would have just been too easy. Besides I truly did want to traverse the same roads I had previously only passed by motor vehicle.

Starting from Valence I intended to cycle up into the Vercors and visit the Grande Goulets a road I have only seen pictured but looks pretty spectacular, following a loop through the Alps I thought it would be fun to visit Alpe D'Huez and having seen photos from the top of the Sarrene that was on the list too. The Cime de la Bonette as the highest paved road in France looked like it would afford top bragging and if I somehow dropped from there on a nice squiggly route then the Verdon Gorge is a suitably gorgeous place to spend a few hours.

Although this route got me no closer to Lourdes, heading as it did in the wrong direction, it does make the mileage up, and give me mileage I could miss out should I find it all too much.

So which way to head West, well although a little out of the way it seemed rude not to include Mt Ventoux, seen as I was trying to make the tour as impressive as possible and if there is one climb cyclists bang on about then this is it.

So looking at the map, where now to get to Lourdes, hmmm like a drop of the old vino so Chateauneuf du Pape sounds like a good idea, and as it is in the general vicinity Pont Nord.

Originally I then opted to cycle through the Camargue and onto the

Pyrenees, however when I realized the dates I would be passing through coincided with the tour I decided to stay further North and perhaps see the pros.

After entering the Pyrenees all that remained was to take a long winded route to take in the biggy the Tourmalet. Then 22 days later catch the coach in Lourdes, how hard could it be!!

January 2012

Another forum ride was scheduled for the end of January, spending at least 30 minutes a day on the new turbo trainer meant I had no qualms about embarking on another 100km ride.

My attention had now turned to the dreaded kit list, spares, clothes for cycling, clothes for relaxing, cycling shoes, day shoes, wet weather clothes, cooking, eating, washing, sleeping the list was never ending. A new tent bought in the sales, a new sleeping bag and mat at the same time, that was nearly 4 kg. Panniers front and rear, empty they weigh 3 kg in total. Torches, lights, batteries. Food rations, gels what was it all going to weigh?

Drink, I knew I went through gallons of water on the turbo, very little on a ride, but I did usually end up dehydrated. How would I manage for water in the south of France in July? A hydration bladder was the answer, carried in its own backpack it would hold 3 litres but then it would weigh 4 kg.

In total with the bike and when bottles and bladder were full with water the weight I was forcing along would be in the region of 45kg. Too much!

In the end I decided if I could buy food to cook I could buy food to eat, the Trangia and its fuel were out, half the clothing was also abandoned, I could wash clothes at camp sites.

So kit list as it stood

Clothing:

Waterproof Trousers
Waterproof Jacket
Overshoes
Gillett
Arm and Leg warmers
Buff
Cap& Helmet

2 x padded cycling shorts
1 x padded liner ✗
1 x long zipoff trousers
1 x w/proof Baggy short
Thermal tights
Swimming trunks ✗
Sandals
Spd trainers
2 x compression vests
1 x l/s HH shirt
1 x casual shirt
2 x s/s l/w cycling jersey
1 x l/s cycling jacket/ Jersey
Long + short fingered gloves
Tent ✗
Ground sheet ✗
Inflatable mat ✗
Sleeping bag ✗
Silk liner ✗
Earplugs ✗
Blow up pillow ✗
Cycling glasses & Normal glasses
Emergency spokes
Spare brake blocks (4 pairs)
Elastic bands
Zip ties
3 x inner tubes + repair kit
Pump
Tape
Spare chain + 2 quick links
Chain lube
Spare guy rope ✗
Arselard
Multitool
Toiletries + m/f towel
Plastic plate and bowl ✗
Knife/ fork/ spoon combo ✗
Camera + spare battery and memory card ✗
Phone + spare battery

Gps + solar charger
Lights + 1 set spare batteries
Cable lock
Map, pad and pencil
Emergency gels
Isotronic water tablets + sterilising tabs
First aid kit `
Wet wipes
Sun cream
Mossy repellant
Cash/ card
Hydropak ✕

February 2012

The coach has been booked, holidays have been booked, all the equipment has arrived, and the training is still ongoing.

The route has been uploaded to the sat nav, only 5 months to go. Money still rolling in and I have even managed to get the local paper to do a small piece on my venture.

The one complication that I had to address was the sat nav. I was using a Bryton Rider that has a rechargeable battery as opposed to taking AA's. I found a USB AA battery holder that will attach to the satnav and also a solar panel that attaches via usb that can sit on the back of the bike. The problem arose because the charging port on the satnav is not accessible when the thing is mounted on the bars. The only way I was able to overcome this was to cut sections out of the mount and then mount it on a plastic bar extender that sits atop my bar bag holder. This extender also needed a large section dremeling out that as seriously weakened the whole set up. This was then taped and glued but it did mean that the USB power cable has to be force fed through a narrow opening about an inch from the port on the USB and jiggled into position.

March 2012

I have to admit that even with the advantage of being able to see the route that is being cycled the TACX can be boring over any length of time. I was also in two minds as to whether the turbo was harder or easier than real life. Finally the weather improved and it was possible to get back out on real roads.

April 2012

I realised I was running out of time, the six months I had to prepare back in January had now halved, the whole venture was becoming very real. Work colleagues and Royal Mail had pledged around £500 and my internet giving pages had hit around £1000.

As a sister ride to the Season of Mists there was another Audax from Hebden Bridge running early in April, of similar length and intensity 'Spring into the Dales' seemed like good proposition. It all started well, right up until the satnav said 'no'. The organisers had warned of a problem with the road by a ford, so when I reached a ford and saw cyclists in front I thought all was well. Following these cyclists for around 10 miles I eventually caught up with them at a road junction. Asking them if they knew how much further it was back to Hebden Bridge I was informed how would they, know they were on their way home for tea, they lived in Leeds!

My Audax was 115km and included more hills. I needed to make sure the routes I was uploading to the satnav unit were actually being shown correctly rather than as vectored straight lines.

During a forum ride in March one of the other 'cyclechatters' had announced their intention to organise their own ride at the end of April. Starting from near Lancaster and heading to the Hawkshead brewery. Whilst this ride promised to be challenging it would be flatter than previous forum rides I had taken part in, and I did debate about travelling the 70 miles from home to take part. However the route looked interesting and the organiser had some touring experience so I thought it would be good to take my loaded panniers, get his input to my kit list and do the ride partially loaded to start to get a feel for a loaded bike.

The weather was blustery but at least it stayed dry which was an improvement over the previous few weeks. The ride was around 140k with 1500m of climbing, I had the rear panniers loaded on the bike around 16kg + water + bike. Overall it felt good but I needed to test the bike fully loaded especially to see how it handled with front panniers on-board.

May 2012

In for a penny, it really was time to see if I could cycle up a mountain whilst carrying all the equipment I would require to spend three weeks on the road in a foreign country. Where do you find a mountain in or near Bradford? Well Holme Moss at 524m might only be a quarter of the height and distance of Ventoux but it is the best I could do and coupled with the steeper undulations on its approach the 95km and 1500m I planned was about as good as I was going to get.

Setting off from home I felt very self-conscious of the spectacle I must have provided, you don't see many loaded bikes cycling my streets. Still 5 hours later I was back home, still breathing and feeling ok. Even the following morning I was feeling fairly good, not jump on a bike and do it again good, but I figured the adrenalin on tour would see me through.

About this time I read an article in the press about a web site called 'Warm Showers' this was a collection of people all over the world who offered a free bed to weary travels on a pay it back in the future basis, another similar website was also mentioned, Couchsurfing. I started emailing anyone and everyone along my proposed route in the hope of a free bed.

June 2012

I had four weeks left, at the end of the month I would catch a bus that over a period of 24 hours would transport me and my bike over 1000 miles to the south of France. For 3 weeks I would be completely alone with no friends or back up. Scary.

Time for one final forum ride, again packing a couple of panniers to simulate touring I headed into Rutland, not too hilly and with excellent road surfaces, I was probably as fit as I was ever going to be. My trouser size was now a 34" but for some perverse reason I had stopped bothering to weigh myself.

The final ride before catching the bus came in the form of a charity sportive, 100km starting and ending in Hornsea. The weather was wet and windy, the sat nav was playing up, the portents where not good. I was hoping for a time of 3 hours (given the terrain is flatter than a flat thing (314 m of climbing) Given the weather I was happy with 3hrs and 20 mins, all be it on the Giant liberated for the occasion from the TACX.

The last day in June saw me in a layby close to Wakefield trying to figure out how to keep my entire luggage together and twist my handlebars to the required position for transporting. My hand luggage consisted of my fully charged Kindle a few snacks, sat nav and 4ltrs of bottled water ready for filling my bottles in 24 hours.

Success, I received several offers of accommodation along my route and others with loads of info about the best campsites and places to eat, some people are truly generous.

Day 0

What can I say about a 24 hour coach journey?

Bike-express are a Hull based company and Wakefield is the fourth point at which they pick up, consequently when I joined the coach it was practically empty affording me the luxury of spreading out over two seats rather than restricting myself to the window seat I had been allocated.

Unfortunately as the journey progressed the coach started to fill up and I was forced into my given place, whilst the reclining seats do afford an amount of comfort and leg space is very good for a coach, at 6'1" I would have preferred ideally to be in an aisle seat.

The coach is well equipped with DVD and toilet facilities and an on-board steward patrolling with the sale of food and drink. The food, whilst microwaved on board, does start as fresh cooked home produce created by the stewards' wife, and for anyone thinking of travelling it is pretty darned good and excellent value. After watching the steward running up and down the coach it wasn't until I stood up and cracked my head on the ceiling that I realised that he wasn't 6'1"!!!

By the time we reached Gravesend that I decided that the seats really were not comfortable at all. A few months earlier I had managed to bruise my coccyx whilst riding a recumbent trike and the seats where moulded in such a way that pressure was being placed on the very area that had been affected. At this point I was seriously questioning whether I would be able to cycle at all!!

On arrival at Dover the couple we were due to collect were not to be seen, with the ferry boarding in about an hour the steward finally made phone contact only to find that they were under the impression it was the next day the coach was due! After explaining they had the arrival date (in France) mixed up with the departure date they then expected the coach to wait 4 hours for them to travel to Dover. NON was the polite version of the answer they received!

Finally on board the early evening ferry, I waved blighty goodbye and found a comfy seat corner to finally lie down and get an hours kip, before returning to the coach for the overnight journey to the South.

Day 1

Sleeping fitfully due to discomfort, and the fact the coach was stopping every hour or two for driver changes, drop offs, fuel etc I was awoke at 6am to be told my pre-ordered sausage sandwich was ready and we would be arriving in Valence in about 40mins.

The view from the coach window was not inspiring, rather than sun drenched fields it was overcast and not looking particularly warm. Pulling into an industrial estate on the outskirts the coach deposited me and 2 others in the car park of an air conditioning factory. My 2 associates were cycling by tandem which had to be lowered carefully from the top deck of the trailer, collecting my baggage whilst this was going on, it wasn't until I noticed the steward climbing back on-board the coach that I realised that he had forgotten to unload my trusty steed. Gesticulating wildly as the coach started to pull away it would have been a very short bike ride had the driver not seen my frantic waving!

Propping my now liberated bike against the side of the building I started to transfer my various bits and pieces.

Front panniers containing tools and bike bits, wet and cold weather clothing, hydration and water purification tablets and the bag of muesli I had packed for breakfast (liberally coated in banana flavoured whey).

Rear panniers containing all clothing, kindle, wash kit and paper map.

Atop the rack was the tent wrapped in a thin waterproof 'ground sheet' strapped on with bungee cords, topped with a solar panel, the cable from which was twined around the top tube and the stem.

Bar bag and extender, around 1200 euros, passport, phone, various batteries and usb battery charger. The sat-nav was connected to the solar charger atop the bar extender after a lot of fiddling with the wires and a camera in a pouch hung from the carrying strap on the bar bag. Bottles in cages, one water, one crammed with Gels, hydration pack filled with bottled water and electrolyte tabs. Sorted, ready to go.

I had studied google earth and google maps as well as cycling this first day already in virtual reality on the TACX so cycling through an industrial estate came as no shock and I was happy to cycle on without paying much attention to the sat-nav that I had initiated when installing it on the handlebars. It wasn't until a couple of miles into the ride that I realised it was not making its customary bleeping noise to signify the next turn, glancing down I found it had turned itself off!!

Now I knew the routes were all loaded correctly having learnt my lesson on the last audax, the unit had been left charging overnight before catching the coach but it was possible the battery was flat as it does have a penchant for turning itself on and flattening the battery, but surely the solar panel should be working? Stopping I re-booted the unit and saw that the battery level was at maximum and that the route was loaded and my physical position matched the map location, mild panic as to why it had glitched, never mind I still had a map, if not any great ability to use it!

The weather remained overcast and that wonderfully British term 'mild'.

The last act before leaving had been to service the bike, oil, grease, lubricate, and tighten. Somewhere I had read about how much damage a loose Bottom Bracket can cause so being ham fisted I had managed to tighten mine up a bit, of course then I read about the catastrophic consequences of an over tightened Bottom Bracket.

Heading into the Vercors between vast fields of wheat, or maybe corn (a farmer I am not) picking up the pace to take advantage of the flat, the first thing I could feel was a grating on each pedal stroke. Had I over tightened that BB? All I could think of what if? How will I? Where is there a bike shop?

In the mid distance low hills shrouded in mist started to materialise, coupled with loud retorts of thunder my mind was soon diverted from any mechanical issues.

Anyone who has cycled will know that waterproofs are the invention of the devil, cumbersome, or flappy, no matter how good, expensive, well fitting, light, you will always end up as wet with them on as off due to the 'boil in the bag' effect. For this reason I tend to put off putting waterproofs on, I usually put this off until am so wet there is no point wearing the damned things in any case. Today it was only going to be a light shower, the storm was miles away, besides which the temperature was starting to rise, and this was the South of France in July, what where the odds of freezing?

Starting my first climb, a proper French climb I felt good, I had no idea what the gradient was, or what the 'hill' was called but I thought to myself, "if this is as bad as it gets then it is going to be an easy holiday." Considering I had very little sleep or food in the last 24 hours I was happy with my own analysis. Oh dear, maybe I hadn't taken into account adrenalin/excitement/ unadulterated panic, call it whatever.

After a about 5 miles of climbing the burn was starting to set in, nothing really can prepare you for a long climb, other than a long climb, but I still manage to plod on without resorting to 'granny gear.' (Which now due to having had to push once too often on forums rides in the distant past, and a bit of fettling/expenditure, was now a tiny 24t chain ring coupled to a massive 11-34t rear cassette.)

In the distance the thunder had finally died down but the mist was starting to meet my upward progress, although dressed only in shorts and cycling top the exertion from the climb was keeping me nice and warm. One thing I had become accustomed to very quickly was the lack of traffic, once I had left the last town behind on the outskirts of Valence I had not seen a single car, in fact the only person I saw at all was a cyclist as he passed me. It was quite a shock that nearly sent me from my bike when two mountain bikes suddenly appeared from the tree line to ride across my path, over the road only to plunge once again into the deep foliage. Stopping to look, there was what to my eyes looked like a shear drop but was obviously a well-worn path snaking between trees only feet apart, these people where complete and utter nutters!!

The mist was getting much thicker, maybe it was time to start thinking about a jacket, but I was already wet so what was the point? Rounding a bend I found myself at the summit of my first French Col. The Tourniol at 1145 meters. Yippee I had just ascended to twice the height I had ever previously ridden, I had all my gear with me, and I didn't feel exhausted, I could do this, I couldn't be far from my resting place for the night and it must be downhill from here!!

In retrospect (which came about 2 mins later, and about every 2 minutes until I reached level ground) I should have put my waterproof leggings and jacket on. In fact I should have put on arm and leg warmers as well. Of course I didn't, they would have got wet and I was stopping in a tent. The descent from the Tourniol was cold, so cold I was starting to get worried. I was starting to worry I was going too fast as well. My brakes weren't coping with the weight they had to stop, the wet rims didn't help. I argued with myself that it was a purpose built tourer and that for years people had ridden these roads with canti brakes safely and securely, it didn't do much to persuade me as once again I tried to slow down with numb fingers for a sharp corner on a wet slippery road with a cumbersome bike beneath me, the grating noise as the pads looked for something to grip on was alarming.

As soon as I felt the gradient slacken I brought the bike to a complete halt and quickly donned a waterproof jacket, I was frozen to the core, not only can't you prepare for long ascents, it is difficult to appreciate the chill felt on a long descent without experiencing it first-hand. Stood underneath a tree the only human being within a goodly radius I started to worry about my physical well being, what if I did freeze, catch hypothermia, who would ever find me? Consulting sat nav (which mercifully was now working without fault) I worked out I had only travelled about a third of my allotted distance and climbed only 700m of the 1800 I was due. Ouch, maybe this holiday would be my last.

Thinking about my options, turning round was pointless, I had passed no habitation since starting the climb so I might as well push on and hope for the best, at least moving would warm me up.

The route I had chosen took me straight from the Tourniol and onto the Col de la Bataille higher than the Tourniol at 1313m not only did I have those 200m to climb but also the 700m or so that I had just lost descending. Fortunately it was milder at the lower altitude and I soon warmed up as the climb started again. I thought I had found salvation as I came across signs for some sort of park and a building appeared out of the mist, along with a car park containing a couple of vehicles if no sign of life. Reaching the building it was indeed a kiosk come café, relief was short lived, like so many other places I was to come across in France it was shut. Whether this was due to my trip being out of season or because of a lack of trade????

Reaching the summit of the Bataille I am sure I would have been rewarded with a magnificent view had I been able to see more than a few yards for the persistent low cloud that was now starting to precipitate in the form of rain. Despite the poor visibility it was obvious that the road was flanked to one side by a steep drop off and that the road was not exactly wide, this didn't do anything for my confidence on the long descent awaiting me. I had already vowed I would stop at the first available opportunity rather than continue to my destination so onward and downward, with just a very quick stop to photo the brown summit sign.

Unfortunately the descent was short lived before heading up the next, the Col de la Rama at 1279m, with the weather getting worse I could not have faced a drop only to have to earn every meter back. As it was a couple of kilometres into the climb I passed a dilapidated and ancient touring caravan parked into the foliage at the roadside, probably used by hunters I was sorely tempted to break in and shelter until the weather improved. In fact the only thing that stopped me was the thought that it probably was no drier inside and starting a fire would be a nonstarter.

Maybe the guys back on Cyclechat had been right, Day 1 was too long, talk about a trial by fire, despite studying the route I hadn't appreciated I would be climbing five Cols even if they were relatively minor compared to some I was planning, their cumulative effect was murderous.

Remembering the Gels I had packed into one of my bottles I devoured one before heading up the Col de la Portette 1175m. The cloud was now above me but the rain was still persistent, riding through forested areas would have been a great assault on the senses had it not been for the lousy weather. The decision not to put on waterproof trousers was not a mistake I would make again as every turn of the pedal was a monumental effort. Not wanting to put further mockers on my doldrums by looking at the distance left I eventually stole a glance at the sat nav 10km to go.

Unfortunately it also meant another climb, the Col de la Chau at 1337m the highest point today but only 225m from the foot of the Portette. Onward and upward, a warm bed and superb French cooking awaited, sod camping for a game of soldiers, the finest hotel would be mine, and the rain was abating!

At the summit of the Chau stood a complex, I stopped and debated, was it open, the entrance stood atop a flight of stairs, leaving the bike at the foot I climbed up and looked in. No sign of life, was this some sort of holiday apartment block, No sign of a tariff just posters for skiing, and it looked expensive!

Off to the side were tennis courts and a few closed and boarded chalets that could be campsite offices or kiosks, whichever, no sign of life. As the rain started and in a bloody minded mood I decided the place was closed and headed downhill for the final few km into my destination town Vassieux-en-Vercors.

By now I could have been wrung out, I doubt I have ever been so wet, so dumping my bike in the doorway and walking into the crowded bar on the outskirts of town was probably not the best introduction to the entire towns population I could have made. It appeared that I had gate crashed a wedding reception, a wedding reception that had been in full swing for several hours. I think even the barmaid was completely out of her tree. Not happy at having left my bike (with all my money and belongings attached) in the middle of a crowd of intoxicated revellers I was struggling to make any sense of what I was saying or being told. Obviously I must have been quite a sight dripping water from every orifice onto every surface I came into the vicinity of. Coupled with my prepared French get me out of trouble phrase, "Pardon, je suis desole, mon Francais est terrible, avez vous une chambre pour la nuit?"

Well this must have sounded amusing to the town wagg at the bar, who it had to be said was probably the town alcoholic as the answer that issued forth provided the other 100 or so guests with much merriment and was delivered at such a speed I caught not a word. Eventually stepping outside under the awning a kindly youngster offered the information that there was a boarding house on the next corner, result.

Pushing the bike with rain pounding I managed to walk the 200 yards indicated to a large house on the corner of the street, it was set back and in its own mini courtyard with a flight of steps up from the roadside, using my last reserves of strength I managed to lift the bulk of my bike and equipment up onto the patio and pushed through the entrance into the 'reception'. Sure enough there was a kind of reception desk but no one in attendance, at least the signs indicated I was indeed in a Chambre Hautes. After shouting 'Pardon' at increasing volume I was rewarded with the lady of the house, at least she wasn't at the wedding party I thought, as I unleashed my favourite French phrase. She was very apologetic, she hadn't provided B&B for nearly 12 months since an elderly relative moved in, I think. She did however point out an hotel across the street that might be open if I hurry as they tend to shut when there is no custom.

No joke, entering the hotel it was shut, everyone was evidently at the wedding and the bar was closed only the reception desk was open. Yes sir we have a room and you can put your bike in the garage, it is heated and here is the key. Sorry sir it is Sunday we don't do food on a Sunday nor breakfast on Monday. As they relieved me of my 65 Euros my look of despondency must have rung a bell as a few moments later the receptionists' helper returned with a tray containing a jug of milk tea, coffee, and some breakfast biscuits. For this gourmet offering I was relieved of a further 10 Euros!!

Wheeling the bike into the garage I was grateful to find it lit and containing the hotels central heating system so at least everything would dry out. Examining the panniers, the front Ortliebs had been a sound investment but the Carradrys had succumbed to some water ingress, fortunately I had the foresight to pack everything in plastic liners so all was good. Grabbing toiletries and dry clothes for morning I headed to my room.

The room was warm and comfortable and the shower hot. After enjoying a shower I soaked in the bath, for a total of 75 euros I was going to get my monies worth! Sitting on the bed I made the most of breakfast, the first food I had eaten since a microwaved sausage sandwich 12 hours, 85km and 1800m+ earlier. The restaurant across the street had not opened and the rain was getting heavier, not a night for exploring. Dragging myself from the bed I rinsed my wet clothes out in the bathroom sink and having wrung them out hung them to dry on the various radiators. My shoes where another problem altogether, not having any spare cycling shoes meant these had to be dry for morning at any cost. Removing the insoles I spent a happy hour with the complimentary hairdryer in the bathroom drying them, it only cut out from overheating twice.

My final act was to check my daily log on the sat nav, no sooner had I turned it on than it died. In my confused and tired state I didn't grasp that the solar panel didn't work without sun and the battery was flat, I decided I would be navigating by map and collapsed into bed.

Day 2

Waking up and looking out of the hotel window was not an inspiring sight, the rain was still pounding down and rivers of water were running along the street outside the door. At least I wouldn't have to make a decision about waterproofs, they would be on from the off.

Having been told that there would be no one in the hotel until 10am and if needed to post the room and garage key in the next door house I knew there was no point searching out further breakfast supplies so the first item on the agenda was to dig out the muesli I had stashed in the panniers and use up the remaining milk provided last night.

Entering the garage it seemed like a good idea to sort the bike out there and then so the panniers were repacked and hung on the racks, and the bike given a quick check over, brakes adjusted and all parts sprayed down with GT85. Reclaiming the waterproofs and the battery holder I headed back to the bedroom. Turning on the sat nav it was indeed a flat battery and plugging in the USB battery pack soon had it fired into life and the days route displayed. One thing I did note was yesterdays temperatures recorded by the device a low of 9°, South of France in July my arse.

Originally I had wanted to cycle the Grande Goulets, a road hewn out of the rock face that plunged down to river level and back up again, however research showed the road had been closed a couple of years earlier for repair and never re-opened, even pedestrian access was now prohibited and the alternative road tunnel didn't appeal on a poorly lit bike.

My alternative was to still cycle the Combe Laval a similar proposition but much higher, a drovers road that was carved from the rock hillside in a process that took nearly 40 years to complete back in the late 1800's, and then descend to my destination via Gorges de la Bourne.

Happy with my route and having consumed a bowl of muesli and whey powder (actually quite tasty) I layered up including over trousers, jacket and overshoes. Today I was aiming to stay warm, dry might be pushing it, the weather forecast on the TV last night showed nothing but rain for the next 4 days in the areas I would be cycling.

Tucking the battery pack into a plastic bag and sealing it against the elements I fitted it on to the bike in place of the solar panel, posted the hotels keys and set off out into the wet and gloom of a Monday morning.

As soon as I exited the town the road started to head upwards the Col de Proncel at 1100m quickly followed by the Col de Carri 121m. It would have been nice to get a few miles under my belt before having to climb continually but with no choice my muscles were soon burning. The rain continued to pound down and as the exertion of the climbs took its toil I started to 'boil in the bag' inside my many layers of waterproof material.

By the time I reached the Col de la Machine I was ready to call it quits, not even a third of the way into my daily grind the rain was making riding (particularly descending) dangerous, the low cloud was removing any sort of visual stimulation from the views, I knew existed from photographs, none existent. At the summit of the Col there is an hotel, pulling over and taking shelter in a car port I decided to examine the map and find the quickest easiest route to some sun, head south and hope for the best by the easiest route and sod everything, Hire a car or van, bung the bike in the back and head directly for three weeks holiday in Lourdes. I would bunk down here for the night. Well I would have, until I saw the prices, discomfort in the wallet overrides physical tiredness every time, besides surely it would be mainly downhill, and how long could the rain bloody last!

The descent along the Combe Laval was possibly the scariest thing I had done to date. I knew the road was cut from a sheer rock face and from photos the drop off the side was several hundred feet, the cloud/mist hung just below the level of the road hiding the magnificent view but somehow making it all the more ominous. The wall at the side of the road separating the traveller from this drop cannot be more than two feet high making it about as much use as a chocolate fire guard. The rain was continuing to pound down with the only respite coming in the form of short tunnel sections where the rock face bulged out. As I was now in complete freefall travelling at insane speeds without the need to pedal further thought turned toward my weedy brakes.

Whilst cleaning the bike the previous night I had wiped a goodly amount of black gunk from around the blocks and had to adjust the brakes inwards due to excessive wear, now I was descending faster than previous and in conditions just as bad. The grating noise had returned and in my minds eye it sounded like metal on metal. Cycling colleagues had told me tales of wearing out sets of brake blocks on road bikes on one wet descent let alone on a touring bike, I was seriously concerned about my ability to slow down enough to negotiate some of the corners.

Fortunately descending at such a rate had the bonus effect that I soon left the cliff face behind and was travelling on slightly less steep road through forested hillside. The downside was that the corners where frequent and sharp, not ideal. Offering a short prayer I found myself cycling through the meadowland of the valley and even caught a glimpse of a weak sun.

A short climb and I entered the town of Pont-en-Royans. This is an ancient and very picturesque town even in the drizzle, the old houses look like they are about to collapse and built out over the river valley with balconies on stilts I am sure they would be condemned by the Health and Safety brigade in the UK. In fact I was not quite sure if there had been an accident or it was some sort of club but there were divers in full wet suits and aqualung gear in the river, but no sign of the officialdom that I would have associated with the French had this been something sinister, it just struck as very odd given the weather conditions.

As the rain had now more or less abated a café on the corner with outside tables under an awning seemed like the perfect respite. Being very English I ordered a nice cup of tea only to be presented with a large box containing around 50 varieties of tea bag on strings, I think coffee in future, less complicated. I wished I wasn't so tight, every time I embark on anything I promise myself I won't worry about money, however having paid nearly £2 for a cup of tea I just couldn't bring myself to find another £5 for a sandwich, however hungry I was from lack of breakfast, a cup of tea and the remainder of some granola bar brought from the UK would have to suffice.

Cracking on, the Gorge was naturally all uphill, travelling as I was in the opposite direction to the raging torrent that was the river Bourne. The road hugs the side of the Gorge mostly at river level with mighty concrete overhangs protecting the traveller from the bombardment of rocks and detritus that are continually washed from the sides. Whilst this offered shelter from the continued downpour moving between these protective canopies entailed cycling through a practical water fall as the rain also cascade from the side edges. Another road I vowed to return to on a warm day as again the views would be incredible.

Leaving the protection of the Gorge the road remained on a slight uphill gradient but became more populated as I headed towards the next town. The rain finally stopped, leaving a murky grey day with low cloud, in the distance a group of cyclists where exiting from what appeared to be a large guest house, thinking that they had probably been unsuccessful in their quest for accommodation I continued to follow them. Despite the rain having stopped I had already decided that a warm bed was on the cards for the night rather than the tent, besides my gear needed drying again.

Entering the town of Lans-en-Vercors and into a picturesque traditional French market square I came across the cycling group milling around as their leader was returning from the towns hotel reception, heart sinking, there must have been nearly 14 of them, I thought they would have booked out the entire place. Joining the group I discovered they were all English and were on a day ride and had been searching somewhere to provide a late lunch. After being invited to join them for a meal of Bolognese which the hotel had agreed to provide I politely declined explaining I was actually looking for a bed for the night.

At least this hotel had an open restaurant and did breakfast! After enquiring about my bike I was given the key to a cellar room in which to lock it. Quickly grabbing the requisite gear I headed to my room passing an open laundry room door, jackpot. Showering and changing into dry clothes I once again hung my waterproofs over the bath and propped the hair dryer in such a way to dry my soaked shoes and insoles. Taking a bag of wet, smelly cycling clothes I headed off to the laundry room, unfortunately my French let me down and instead of the maid quickly bunging everything in the dryer I was directed to reception to organise the service.

Being a tight arse I wasn't keen on what this was likely to cost, nor did I fancy my best shorts being boil washed and blasted with detergent, but the thought of having to wear them again overcame even my resistance. How they were washed I never found out but they were returned smelling slightly fresher if not a great deal dryer. Whether this service was free to all guests, or it was because I had so few items, or maybe they just felt sorry for me, either way there was no charge when I came to pay the bill the next day.

Warm, dry and wearing fresh clothes, the rain a memory, I set off to explore the town, the square is more or less it from what I saw, sitting as it does in a depression and on this occasion completely ringed by low cloud, back to the hotel then and time to service the bike. The cellar I had been allocated had some lighting, not nearly enough for my purpose, with hindsight it would have been sensible to move outside to change the rear brake blocks, but nearly 30 minutes later and a lot of swearing the bike was cleaned, oiled and sporting a new set of pads. The old pads where completely shot, I say old, they were new 2 days ago.

I knew the cellar wasn't my own private domain, it contained a couple of other bikes and a large chest freezer, and obviously had access from an internal door, but when I booked in I had been given the key to the door as well as one for my room, how was I to know I had the only spare key to the outside cellar door? Entering the lobby and being accosted by the manager I was informed they had been trying my room for the last hour for the keys return, a member of staff needed his bike from the cellar to get home, sorrrrry.

The rest of the evening was uneventful, the three course meal included in the room rate was very welcome if nothing to write home about, and the weather forecast was more of the same. The next day I would have to make a decision, head directly south from Grenoble down the route Napoleon to pick up my itinerary around the Verdon Gorge or continue to head east into the high Alps.

Day 3

Pulling back the curtains I was not expecting much from the day. The low cloud that had ringed the town the previous evening had if anything grown thicker with visibility down to 200 yards. In the market square a couple of traders were beginning to set up stall, giving the impression that they were the only ones that had been bothered on this day. I headed down to breakfast, the first person to arrive in the dining room I had the full choice of warm croissants and pastries, bread rolls, ham, cheese and boiled eggs. Having eaten my fill I surreptitiously filled a few bread rolls with ham and cheese as well as pocketing a couple of hard boiled eggs, at least food on the days journey was not going to be hard come by.

The road out of Lans was a steady climb of about 3% for the first 9 km, starting off through lightly forested hillside that gave way to open meadowland before the drop into Grenoble. As I ascended the cloud ascended with me so I never faced the wet slog I was expecting, and it was a relief to stop and remove the waterproofs, remembering to replace the jacket with a gillet for the descent into the cities outskirts.

As with all sat navs maps do go out of date so it was of little surprise to find myself trying to cycle the wrong way down a one way street, what came as a little more worrying was being told to turn into someones drive and cycle through their house. Trying to work out an alternative route in a populated area using a 2" screen is not for the faint hearted, nor is riding through large cities environs in a foreign country with alien road signs and lane priorities, whilst using the same 2" screen. This was the point I must make up my mind, South or East.

With the weather now seemingly defying the forecasters and not fancying my chances of actually finding the route Napoleon I opted to follow my original plans, when the sat nav appeared to send me down an autoroute slip road my resolve did slip until I noticed the well-worn cycle lane markings. Finally exiting the mayhem I was on the main road to the Alps.

Not having to worry about any further directions until the turn off for Allemond I was able to relax after the pressure and tension I had allowed to build up in the City. The road was smooth, only a slight gradient and the low cloud was staying out of the valley and hugging the tree lined slope in the distance, there was even signs that the sun might put in an appearance. The best sign though was a large electronic road sign listing the various Cols in the area all with the Ouvert glowing.

Following the road into the next valley I started the slightly steeper ascent toward the town of Allemond and by the time the turn off for the town itself came into sight the sun was out at full force. Signs outside the pharmacy in Lans had recorded the Temp at 13°, whilst here in Allemond it was a barmy 28°, at last my 'holiday' could start.

This turn of fortune also meant it was time to crack out the tent, I knew I had two choices of campsite in Allemond, the first I passed by, being a complete midge magnetic I decided against camping in a ring of trees and opted instead to stay in the Municipal facility directly below the dam and the start of the climb up the Glandon and Croix de Fer.

After the expense of the previous two nights it was a nice surprise to be asked for only 6 euros for a nights camping as a cyclist. Picking a prime position and pitching the tent for the first time I off loaded everything but the bar bag from the bike and examined my options. It was only noon and my original intention (flight of fancy) had been to cycle the Croix de Fer that afternoon before heading over the Lauteret the next day via the Alpe D'Huez and the Col de Sarrenne. I had other options for the next day rather than this high pass, I could use the various balcony roads to Le Freney-d'Oisans from the Alpe or indeed the main Valley road.

I had of course read all about the Alpe d'huez and the Glandon, I had watched videos of cyclists on the Sarrenne I had studied the profiles of them all, I knew the Lautaret was 34k of solid uphill, it would be unlike anything I had tackled so far by multiples, in my heart I knew I didn't stand a chance of linking three major climbs in one day.

I wanted to tackle the Croix de Fer, I had cycled it many times on the TACX with real life video, it looked magnificent and with the sun shining and my gear back at the tent I knew I could do it, however I had no spare time, I had to tackle the Lauteret in the morning to meet my schedule. I couldn't return home having not climbed the Alpe d'Huez, this was more of a trophy climb than any other.

Decision made I saddled up and headed up the face of the dam, instead of turning left and up the Croix I turned left and headed to Villard-Reculas on the D44b balcony road to Huez. It was a long steep slog in the 28° heat, the road was twisting and no more than a car width wide, the drop sheer into the valley below, only separated by a waist high wood pole fence. Despite only riding for an hour I had exhausted the single water bottle I had elected to carry, unaccustomed and un-acclimatised to riding in this new found heat. Rounding a bend the twisting ribbon of tarmac that is the Alpe d'huez road appeared shimmering below me, I was looking down on the famous numbered bends, so in my mind I had more than achieved this trophy climb.

Of course that was an illusion, the balcony road actually comes out in Huez village five or six corners below the actual summit, but I was spent, there was a water fountain to fill my bottle and drink my fill. Even with the bike stripped down to a measley 20kg or so I just couldn't face the extra climb, dropping from Huez I also realised I hadn't faced a proper descent before now. Serious gradients meant serious speed, hairpin bends, proper switchbacks, meant a need to lose that speed.

Having read scary tales of exploding tyres from heat build up when braking I was very conscious of my inability to descend at speed, it's a confidence thing, and stopping every corner to pour water from my one bottle onto my rims probably gave every other serious cyclist that day a good laugh. My lack of confidence wasn't helped by the amount of traffic, for the first time since landing in France with the exception of Grenoble I was also having to fight for road position with cars, cars that could brake a lot harder than I could.

Flattening out onto the main road from Bourg-d'Oisans back to

Allemond came as some relief, whilst my confidence in my abilities had increased the lower I had got I was still nervous about the mechanical capabilities of my brakes, I knew it was something I needed to overcome as longer and steeper descents faced me.

I couldn't work out where they had come from, the road surface was smooth tarmac, but the shoulder and cycle lane were littered with small stones or flint another cyclist had suffered a puncture whilst a second was riding along crouched over his bars, his hand resting on the front tyre as a brushing bar to remove these small stones as they stuck to his tyre. Luckily no catastrophe befell me but on returning to the camp I spent a happy 15 minutes picking particles out of the tyre treads. I guess this was an advantage of running touring tyres.

Having remembered to use sunscreen this afternoon I was happy to laze out in the warmth of the late afternoon reading my kindle, probably the best 'unnecessary' weight I could have carried. The sat nav had powered down in Huez so I left this out in the full sun attached to the solar panel in the hope it would be charged for tomorrow, with all the bad weather I was rapidly running out of batteries.

Having dozed off I woke with a rumbling stomach and decided it was time to find a place to eat. From what I saw Allemond is basically one road. In the town centre there are a couple of cafes that didn't look very appealing to get a substantial meal, a boulangerie, which was closed for holidays, and a Pizzeria. On my arrival I had noticed a Pharmacy, a Spa shop and a couple of promising buildings that looked like hotels. Walking the mile or so to the main road and the location of the 'Welcome to Allemond' sign I called into the Spa, it is a tiny general store with general provisions, not having any intention of making a meal I opted for a can of coke and a banana, the one solitary banana cost over £1. From here on in I wouldn't be relying on bananas for energy.

The walk had proved fruitless (with the obvious exception of the banana), one hotel was closed down, and going to seed, the crazy golf in the garden overgrown and covered in weeds. The other building advertised a menu outside but was shut and evidently going the same way as the first. A third was open, the prices where on the steep side and the menu uninspiring, pizza it was going to be.

What a revelation, ordering a large beer was a god send, the second equally so and about time to look at the menu. Ordering a salad for what I thought was a starter and a large pizza along with a litre pitcher of red vino tonight was looking up. In fairness I think the waitress thought I was expecting company, maybe it was the litre of wine? But the pizza and salad arrived at the same time and on equally massive plates, explaining that the salad was a starter an oo la la later I was tucking into a delightful salad that was followed by an exquisite pizza. Maybe I am easily pleased, or maybe I was slightly merry but that was one hell of a meal and collapsing into my tent half an hour later I fell sound asleep, not even worried that my bike was leant against a tree in the middle of nowhere.

Day 4

The day dawned bright and beautiful, the weather monsieurs had got it wrong! Having said that the camp site was in shade being overlooked by the grass bank of the hydro dam and the valley walls to the East and West.

Today was going to be my most stressful, I had a big climb ahead, and I had to locate a house in a small hamlet belonging to a single lady who spoke no English but had agreed to give me a bed for the night.

It started badly, my wife had bought me an expensive watch in the past and for some unknown reason I had decided it would be perfectly safe to go cycle touring with it. Returning from my morning ablutions I couldn't find it anywhere. Panic set in scouring the toilet block, no result. Chasing around the campsite questioning everyone that was awake if they had found a watch, no result. Talking to the site warden, no result.

Admitting it wasn't worth going home now and I would have to forever live in my tent on foreign soil I morosely started to de-camp, my watch fell out of the sock I had stuffed it in for safe keeping the night-before, with a light head I jumped on my trusty steed (that had also made it through the night) and singing a happy tune cycled off in the direction of the Lautaret.

I got to the main road before the sat-nav beeped and gave up the ghost, the solar panel had put absolutely no charge into the battery despite being in bright sun for over 3 hours, unpacking the USB battery pack I inserted my last batteries, 2 AAA that were spares for my rear light. I thanked my lucky stars that the battery pack accepted both AA and AAA and once again set off.

Ignoring the roundabout exit to Bourg-d'Oisans I had made up my mind that the Lautaret would be my only climb today, and what a climb at 34km and around 1400m it promised to be a long long drag from the valley to the summit.

The climb starts from Le Clapier and seems relatively innocuous. Riding though the first of many tunnels it soon became apparent that this was a main road as trucks and lorries hurtled towards me there headlights providing the only light. Reaching the end I decided it would be a good idea to at least switch on my lights for the rest of the day!

Riding over the dam at the end of the Lac du Chambon it disappears snaking into the distance and it wasn't until I had climbed along its Northern edge that I realised how big it was, the road, again with a very low barrier wall soars for miles over the vast flood plain exposed from the lack of run off after a mild winter. The road eventually drops to meet the Romanche river before once again ascending alongside the rivers course providing glimpses of the torrent through the trees lining the road.

The next obstacle I faced with trepidation was the tunnel De Grand Clot, the sign at its entrance advises that it has a gradient of 3.6% and is ½ km long. The noise and heat emanating from its mouth makes you think you are entering the gates of hell. Making sure my lights were all working and waiting for the arctic below me to pass by I eventually plucked up courage to navigate this behemoth. Screams where renting the air as I was barely a third of the way through, thinking there had been some horrendous accident I was both relieved and slightly annoyed to see a group of cycling lights approaching me at fantastic speed, the riders whooping and hollering as they descended through the darkness.

I don't know whether this is a good or bad thing but many climbs in France have signs every kilometre advising riders how far they have to travel and the average gradient they can expect for that section. On the Lautaret the gradient gets gradually steeper. Even 3.6% seems like a sheer rock face after 20 or so kilometres without respite, so seeing signs for 6, 7 and 8% has a demoralising effect, when coupled with 26° heat and being told there is still 14k to go the pedals seem to rotate through treacle.

I passed through a couple of towns, but every visible café appeared full, or closed, I had my hydration pack but the water inside was now luke warm from the heat of the sun and body heat from my sweating back. For breakfast I had a helping of my muesli and I still had a small amount of the granola slab I had from the UK. In all honesty I needed a rest and my bloody minded attitude to conquering this mountain in one was not going to help. I committed myself to stopping at the next town, village, hamlet whatever.

This turned out to be Villar-d'Arene, ironically but unbeknown to me only a short ride from the summit (should have taken more notice of those roadside signs!), The wooden shack/kiosk at the side of the road was closed, the expensive looking posh hotel restaurant with veranda mounted tables complete with crisp white linen and parasols was open. Cycling past and turning round my desperation for something cold overcame my tight-fisted nature, besides which I saw a sign saying they sold ice lollies!

Stacking the bike against the veranda support I climbed the steps (I suppose the staff are used to sweaty cyclists but at the time I expected to be politely told to leave) and swerving between the tables entered the cool interior looking for the waist coated and aproned waiter. Asking for a 1 euro ice lolly seemed a little demeaning but to give credit the maître D sent the waitress off to fulfil my order. Sorry sir (in French) we have sold out!

I couldn't face the return to the bike so throwing caution to the wind I asked for a menu, a table for one, and a large jug of iced water. The menu de jour looked interesting whatever it was and I was soon enjoying stuffed squid, I really must learn French. To add insult to injury when paying for the meal I was presented with the ice lolly I had originally asked for and a bill for the extra Euro.

Forty minutes later I found myself at the summit of the Col de Lautaret, surrounded by cyclists and day trippers, an abundance of kiosks selling drinks and nibbles and a large hotel restaurant, never mind the squid wasn't that bad. Not even thinking about attempting the ascent up the Galibier, after a quick photo with the col summit sign I started my descent.

The descent of the Lautaret heading east is a lovely road without the keener hairpin bends associated with many of the other Cols and it was a very swift and fun descent that lasted all too short a time before I was having to brake sharply for what appeared to be a dirt track but what my sat nav told me was the road into La Casset, the hamlet that was the home of Martine my hostess for the night. Following the rutted track I reach a small village with old crumbling houses tightly packed along twisting cobbled streets. Religiously following the sat nav it brought me into an overgrown yard surrounded by houses any one of which could be my bed for the night. Approaching an elderly lady sat out on her porch I enquired after Martine, I think she recognised the name but neither of us understood the other. Cycling to the centre of what was in fact a well-proportioned village with café and church I asked a couple if they could direct me to the address I had been given. They pointed me back where I had just been, giving up I decided a drink was in order before phoning my evening's hostess.

Martine was at work and would return in 3 hours, she would meet me in front of the church, she drove a blue Renault. As far as I could gather.

With three hours to kill I locked the bike and leaving the panniers on trust decided to explore the immediate vicinity. Outside the church a river flowed under an old stone bridge, the river bed was littered with large boulders and the torrent passing over was a cauldron of white rapids, it was with some amazement that I saw a garage door open onto the river only for several canoeists to issue forth into the maelstrom. No thanks!

Eventually I spotted a little blue Renault and remarkably it turned out to be Martine. I was the first person she had ever hosted through the Couchsurfing website and had only signed up for it when her son had left home and used the same site backpacking. As it turned out she lived above the elderly lady in the courtyard, telling me to wheel my cycle into the back garden into a wood store for safety she then showed me her sons' room where I was to sleep for the night. Her son had only recently left, I was informed, and wanted to be a firefighter, the bedroom walls were adorned with posters for ski and mtb events and several trophies dotted the shelves a very sporty young man, and what a place to grow up in!

After a bath and change I was invited to join Martine and her friend on the balcony overlooking (or should that be being overlooked?) by the mountains where we enjoyed a stilted yet convivial conversation over a long beer or two. Martine had also gone to the trouble to cook a meal for myself and her friend, with two women waiting on me how could I not be content? The food was everything I could have hoped for in a French household, a lovely roast chicken with veggies and a potato gratin with a charming sauce. As the chicken was brought to the table Martine stumbled and we discovered the chicken could still fly, luckily it landed in the middle of the table! Cheese and biscuits followed a crème brule and fully sated it was off to a warm comfy bed.

Day 5

I needn't have worried about the protocol, Martine was up and downstairs before I was awake, hot coffee, cheese and buttered fresh bread before a heartfelt thank you and a parting wave. The road out of La casset was obviously the road that was meant to be used being of smooth tarmac compared to the rutted track I had approached on. Although the first few hundred meters out of Casset were uphill the next few km where all easy pedalling into Briancon.

Briancon is an ancient walled city dating back to the Roman Empire, it is the highest city in the EU, and at times it felt like the roads were original as well. Following my trusty sat nav (sic) I was being directed down what appeared to be a back street in a state of utter disrepair. Deciding to ignore the electronics advice, thinking that as the Izoard is a major road out of Briancon I found myself completely lost and heading on to a ring road of sorts, lesson learnt and an about turn. After successfully negotiating the city streets and within literally yards of their hubbub I found myself on a country road that is the start of the Izoard.

This was the first climb I had already experienced by car a few years earlier, I remember that it was a hairy experience on that occasion, particularly the Southern step through the 'Casse Deserte'. A lot of the cycling books and information I had reviewed prior to the trip had advised no stopping in this area due to numerous and frequent rock falls from the barren sides, they went on to say it was best to ascend from the south doing so meant dodging the detritus in the road. In fact descending down this rocky hillside was ill-advised due to the likelihood of gravel on the corners and rocks in your path. Something I could relate to when driving the route. If this wasn't bad enough the books also went on to say whilst the Col was a good climb from the North if descending the same way, the flies could be a problem on slow ascents.

Naturally my route made the ascent from the North and descended to the South.

I was buoyed early in the climb, shortly after leaving Briancon on a

5% section of the climb I smoothly passed a group of cyclists all on lightweight racing machines and in various replica team lycra, as a bonus they all looked younger than me as well, no doubt they knew what lay ahead and where conserving their energy for the much steeper later sections.

Climbing the Izoard from Briancon involves climbing over 1100m in a distance of 19km. The first few km lured me into a false sense of security, in the first half of the climb the road rarely exceeds 5% with only a short section hitting 8% and involves a short section where the road gently undulates, the landscape is mainly meadowland as it meanders through the valley with the hillsides gradually filling out into dense forest. The town of Cervieres lays about midway, nestled in a bend in the road in meadowland on a gentle sloping hillside there are few visual clues to tell you that the gradient is getting steeper, only the increased pressure required to force the pedals round and the burning in my calves told me it was time to drop a cog or two. Along the way there are a few false horizons that block out the view of the full challenge facing one. It is not until the commune of Laus that the full spectacle of the Izoard comes into view. The rising road can be seen to be heading out of the alpine meadowland into a vast forest that ends in a straight line giving way to a grey mountain top, looking like a layer cake of equal proportions. I decided to stop at Laus for few moments and eat the last of my granola slab, fortunately noticing that the wire from the solar pack had become dislodged from the sat nav meaning no power was being fed. I was a little dubious if it was working when hooked up but my batteries were now exhausted and any little would help until I bought some more. The wire was incredibly fiddly to fit into the charging point but stubbornly I refused to dismantle the unit from the bars and eventually got a blinking green light to indicate charge was at least flowing in some direction.

Pushing on I entered the tree line, for the start the trees were set back from the road side and gave no respite from the sun, I was surprised looking at my temperature gauge to find it was only 22° I was starting to find the relentless gradient a real problem. As the trees began to thicken I learnt why the books had warned about flies, they were consistent and persistent, there was no way I could out run them and of course the amount I was perspiring was attracting them from miles around, the only respite coming from the occasional motorcyclist flying past at high speed and causing a draft.

Deciding that a photo break was the answer I stopped to admire the scenery and snap off a few mementos. Giving the muscles a rest I pushed the bike for a few minutes over a particularly steep section of road before attempting to re-mount. Now mounting a touring bike that is loaded to the gills is not the easiest or most elegant thing, once the bike is off vertical the weight of the panniers takes over and having panniers on the front wheel as well pulls the wheel round causing the whole thing to become very unstable. When this is coupled with an 8% gradient and the width of the rear panniers stopping you from cocking your leg over easily then the whole process becomes an ordeal as I soon found out, barely catching the bike as I nearly ended up in a tangle precariously close to the road edge. In future and mounting and dismounting would be done towards the middle of the road, it would be safer!

Setting off on a slope particularly with this weight is not easy either, I was in a low gear 36 x 34 so the half turn of the crank would barely move the bike a yard let alone build up any momentum to get the other shoe clipped in and pedalling after a couple of stalled attempts I managed to adopt a technique of riding diagonally across the road to lessen the effect of the gradient whilst not making the angle I had to turn the wheels too great before hitting the ditch at the inward side of the road. The short walk had a positive effect using a different set of muscles and I felt at ease once I was moving, it is strange when setting off how little effort it seems to take to pedal, compared with the action of continuous pedalling . The ease was short lived, soon my calves and thighs were burning as before but setting myself a target before I thought about taking another photo I continued upward.

I remembered the lower gearing I had fitted after failing on my first audax, though I loathed to have to resort to 'granny' gear on a mere 8% slope I had to do something, but I couldn't change gear. My fingers were rigid, it couldn't be the cold, because it wasn't, I just hadn't moved them from the position on the bars for over an hour, I had been in the same gear with no need to brake and simply hadn't thought about altering hand position, they were completely numb. I wasn't going to stop again yet so trying to manipulate feeling into my hands whilst cycling uphill was probably not the safest option but it worked, dropping into 24x 34 and pedalling became too easy. Using such a low mountain bike gear is a double edged sword as I found out. Cycling with my usual cadence the bike was hardly moving and becoming highly unstable as I had to saw at the bars to keep it upright. The lack of pressure required on the cranks meant I was also gradually pedalling faster and faster, beyond my comfort zone and using up more precious energy and different muscle fibres that weren't accustomed to continual use. I was also aware that if I stopped in this gear on this hill there would be no way I would be able to propel the bike forward with enough momentum in order to set off, stop and I was pushing to the summit.

I had managed to get life back into my hands to change gear from the 36 to 24 chain rings, but of course in this direction the change is spring assisted, the change back from small to large offers much more resistance particularly when already applying large amounts of torque through the drive chain. Nearly crying with the pain and the feeling of complete frustration as I tried to force the lever with my still weakened hand, the only solution was to relieve the pressure on the chain by pedalling like mad and then trying to get the bike to freewheel whilst pedalling slowly, after much exertion I managed to get the higher chain ring and pulled over for a quick 'photo' stop.

Setting off was a little easier this time, whether my technique was improving or the gradient less I didn't bother to think about, and a few minutes later I had climbed out of the tree line and miraculously away from the incessant flies. This side of the Izoard is not quite as barren as it first appears with light grass growing on all but the highest peak, it is obvious you have nearly reached the summit as the corners come closer together, true hairpins, and the odd building visible on their apex.

The Izoard must be an iconic climb, this was my first encounter with the professional memento photographer. Crouching at the edge of the road with his telephoto lens poised as I wobbled past trying to smile he suddenly jumps up racing after me trying to thrust a small square of card into my hand, like a relay runner in a baton change I dexterously reached behind and grabbed his kind offering, managing a breathless merci and not falling off in the process!

Crossing the summit at nearly 2400m I briefly stopped to put on a gillet and arm warmers (having learnt my lesson about wind chill) whilst admiring the marker post commemorating the achievement of the French soldiers who built this passage. Stopping almost immediately on the descent to pay respects at the memorial erected to Tour de France legends Coppi and Bobet, I took a few minutes to study the road snaking below me and made a plan of action. I had to avoid any material in the road, avoid flying off on the hairpin bends that had no guard rails whatsoever and basically avoid dying on these steep barren rock strewn mountainsides.

The plan was to go as slow as possible the whole way down, not care if I got in anyone's way or held them up there was no way I was going to allow my momentum to build up on this road and have to rely on my brakes. To give you an idea please google La Casse Deserte, the sharp rock formations jut out from scree slopes at all angles, the scree slopes appear to have been landslides that have just occurred, the road is dug out of these landslides, and is continually having to be cleared and dug out again and again after each winter, bout of bad weather, or when Mother Nature decides.

The descent through the Deserte lasts for around 3km and sticking to plan I manage to keep my speed to under 30kmh, once the scree slopes are left behind the road keeps the same gradient but the hairpin bends flatten out as it hugs the rocky cliff face down to the town of Arvieux. Here the road plateaus and allows me to scrub off the speed I had now gained without worrying about the brakes, checking later I had reached a heady 62kmh!

The descent of the south side is around 16km before reaching the Combe du Queyras and ending at a turquoise lake. The river feeding this lake from the North and running through the Combe joins the side of the road a few km earlier as the gradient eases and the road is joined by the D947.

The Combe du Queyras road hugs the side of the valley hundreds of feet above the river below, cycling on the right means I am on the valley side of the road and the traffic has increased as I am heading towards the town of Guillestre, though where it came from is a mystery. The 'safety' barrier between me and certain death is a low stone wall 18 inch high that is broken or missing in places, it does afford a magnificent view of the turquoise waters rushing by as it appears directly beneath me, only obscured by the odd gnarled tree clinging to the rocky sides. As the road drops to meet the river a mile or so from my days destination, Guillestre, the river widens into an elongated lake of the deepest turquoise blue, I fantasise that there must be somebody somewhere dyeing the water.

As I approached Guillestre I reached a roundabout, one direction said Guillestre the other pointed to Vars, it was only around 2pm, and the route to Guillestre was downhill. I a moment of madness I decided rather than cycle down into town, only to have to cycle back up the following morning, I would make some time on my itinerary and push on to Vars, or even Jausiers, my next days destination. For somehow in my head I had got the idea that the Col de Vars wasn't particularly long or hard.

Maybe it was seeing its 2100m profile alongside that of the Izoard at 2360m maybe it was its gradient looking flat or maybe, just maybe I didn't appreciate I had descended to 1000m and that the Vars represented a climb of 1100m over 20km in length.

Certainly the first few kilometres climbing at over 8% soon dispelled the myth of ease, with every kilometre cycled I was expecting to see the summit, the road winds uphill through grassland giving the impression you are heading straight up, it isn't until it rounds a final corner and stretches out into the distance that you realise you have a long way to go. In the distance I could see a town and cycling on came across a sign welcoming me to Vars, with relief I believed I had almost reached my goal and that the summit would be only a couple of kilometres in the distance. This sign was a complete misnomer, it should have welcomed me to the Vars district, the town I had seen turned out to be Saint Marcellin de Vars, the next town

Sainte Catherine de Vars and finally Sainte Marie de Vars, nowhere near Vars or Vars summit! The road continued onward and upward into the distance, I was starting to feel hungry having shunned Guillestre I had passed nowhere offering food, the one prospect in the last town had been boarded up. I was well and truly in ski country, and there was no snow, everyone had disappeared for the summer.

I eventually arrived in Vars, a concrete jungle of a street with ski shop and café following ski shop and hotel, most of which were deserted apart from the odd souvenir ski shop. The main road through Vars that homes these establishments is one long sweeping corner the width of the road widens to accommodate on street parking that was deserted, the inner apex a courtyard space for another concrete block of tourist accommodation that reminds me of low rise council flats complete with a shopping precinct below. Investigating further there is indeed a small supermarket, a godsend regardless of the no doubt inflated prices.

Not having any idea now how much further there was to cycle to the summit of this godforsaken mountain I bought supplies, a large bottle of coke, the largest bar of chocolate they had and some batteries for the sat nav that had finally died, an inner part of me praying I was still on the right route and shouldn't have turned off in one of the previous villages!

Firing up the sat nav I discovered I was finally in Vars itself, and that the summit of the Col was only three kilometres distant. Fed on a massive sugar rush of chocolate and Coke, managing to attach the 2 litre pop bottle under a pannier strap I set off for the top. The summit of Vars is approached through a grassy gently sloping meadowland, shortly before the summit I passed a massive crane that wouldn't have been out of place in any inner city, obviously the view in coming years would be ruined as commerce intervened, but for now there where only backpackers with tents rather than skiers with cars and concrete high risers.

The only building for now was a wooden café, originally a refuge built by Napoleon it now served hot drinks and offered sanctuary to weary travellers and tourists alike. Foregoing its attractions as time was now passing I headed for a commemorative photo of the regulation brown sign marking my achievement. Until today I hadn't come across any other cyclist on loaded touring bikes, but today there was a fellow tourist stood by the sign, asking if he would mind taking my photo we soon got chatting. Graham was also from the UK and was following the Route de Grande Alpes over the Bonnet tomorrow and then South to the Med. I explained my error in combining the Izoard with the Vars in one day and amazingly he had done the same thing, even more astoundingly he had met a couple at the foot of the Izoard who were debating on the Guillestre or push on over the Vars quandary and they had cycled up together, they were in the refuge Napoleon recouping over a hot chocolate.

The couple where from Australia and had been touring areas of France for several weeks on a six month sabbatical, they were on real heavy duty touring bikes that made mine look like a racing bike, not envious of their weight I was envious of the disc brakes they sported. Joining us Anne and Dominic were easy to get on with and we instantly had a rapport. Finding out that we all planned on stopping at the campsite in Jausiers for the night we agreed to meet up there for a drink. The descent to Jausiers is slightly longer at over 20km with the steepest gradients being higher than those on the ascent from Guillestre, with their superior braking power and confidence born of time in the saddle the two Aussies had soon left me well behind, with Graham opting to spend more time at the summit I was soon cycling solo once again.

Although we had agreed to meet at the camp site at the base, Dominic had referred to it by name having stayed there before, and whilst he had described its location, the description seemed to relate to several sites I passed on the way to Jausiers. Deciding to push on and trust my own route I resigned myself to my own company.

The campsite in Jausiers is actually someone's back garden and is accessed by passing through the house or down a narrow passage way. The tariff is ridiculously cheap but a warm shower is extra. Entering the garden I found I was in the right place, Anne and Dominic where already pitched up, showered and changed and ready to eat. Telling them I would be a while showering and setting up and that they might as well get off and I would possibly catch them in town.

One thing I had noticed was I was beginning to suffer from knee pain and hoped a hot shower would help, thinking it was the effect of too much climbing. After making camp and showering I began my regular bike maintenance, and found that my saddle was decidedly saggy. I had treat myself to a Brooks Flyer, a leather sprung saddle that was aged for comfort, but with the torrential rain I had experienced over the first two days the leather had stretched causing the sagging and no doubt the pain I was experiencing in my knee and no doubt my saddle was effectively too low. The saddle does have a bolt on a nut under the seat that can be rotated to stretch the leather taut to counteract wear so this was not the end of the world, unfortunately it also comes with a specific spanner to do this which I didn't think to pack, the only spanners I had where of the ring variety and could not be used to access the nut.

Fortunately by this time Graham had arrived so hopefully he would be better equipped. Astounding, I can't imagine the weight the guy must have been carrying but he practically had a full tool roll. No Brooks spanner per se, but a whole selection of ordinary spanners and even two sizes of mole grips! After managing to fit the saddle I invited him to join me at a restaurant but he said he was on a tight budget and opted to cook himself, yup he was carrying a stove and an array of pots and pans.

Walking around another one street town I spotted the Aussies in the only bar, they had already eaten so wishing them good night I headed into the bars rear restaurant and settled down with a well-deserved bottle of red and a three course plate de jour.

Day 6

Today I was tackling the highest paved road in the Alps, at over 2800m the Bonette is a bit of a French con, the last few meters giving it the title is a purpose built road circling the summit, the actual 'pass' road can be traversed much lower. To further enhance this road it is widely advertised as the highest road in Europe, unfortunately this accolade must go to the Spanish and the Pico de Veleta at 3384m it dwarfs the Bonette.

Nevertheless at 24k and 1600m height gain from Jausiers it is not a challenge to be taken lightly, the summit was quite likely to still have snow having only been open officially a short while and its season being short. Previously I had climbed this mountain from the other direction by car and remember it is a very open landscape with magnificent views, there are also many abandoned buildings to explore on its slopes.

If I woke feeling the pains of yesterday I had the option to relax having made a day combining the Izoard and Vars.

As it was I awoke early, Graham had been an even earlier riser and was already setting off as I headed to my morning constitutional, he explained he preferred his own pace and company, who was I to argue, mostly agreeing with him in any case. After a bowl of muesli and filling my water bottles I was ready to go by 8am, the air was cool with the temperature hovering around 10° but the sky was clear and it looked promising. Anne and Dominic were just surfacing and said they were heading to the bar for breakfast so our little group looked to be doomed before it had begun.

The road started to climb shortly after leaving Jausier, the first kilometres passing through farmsteads with long horned goats grazing the hillside, passing a large dog I hoped it would stay snoozing it didn't. Chasing after my bike I started to imagine all sorts of doomsday scenarios from being savaged to rabies, how ironic if I had to end in hospital due to a dog, when the whole enterprise had been to help the hounds! Fortunately we must have reached an invisible boundary and deciding it had sent me packing the dog turned tail and left me to my pedalling. Deciding today to preserve my energy I got into plodding mode and as the road headed ever upward turning from pastureland to a craggy valley with forested rocky slopes, the road wound its way up the valley side the loud crashing noise announced the presence of a magnificent waterfall at the head of the valley over which the road traversed. Taking advantage of my early start I was making many photo stops and pushing the bike to the next bend not wishing to have to dismount again and again to capture the scene.

It was at a point just below the final bend taking the road above the waterfall and out of the valley that Dominic caught up with me, I know I had been travelling slowly but he must have been fair motoring! Of Anne there was no sign, in order not to continually fall out they cycled at their own paces and stopped at agreed waiting points, he wasn't worried about her abilities and didn't expect to see her again until the summit. Over the head of the valley and the road once again cuts through sparsely wooded grassland and finally open grassland with only rocks protruding. The gradient is steady but takes its measure of pain and Dominic is slowly pulling away into the distance and once again I settle into my own meandering pace. Closer to the summit and large abandoned buildings come into view, these are old army barracks that I am sure could be made into a fantastic hotel, if only they wouldn't be under meters of snow 8 months of the year! After passing a lake the summit comes into view. The road can be seen to cut through a narrow gap in a grey embankment, alternatively it continues at an ever increasing gradient around the Cime to give it the title of highest paved road in France. The peak of the mountain from this distance is a flat grey shingle reminding me of a coal slag heap, the sides are steeply sloping and the road has no safety barriers whatsoever, from the direction I am approaching I will be cycling on the outer edge and descending on the outer edge, deciding that this was stupid I took the cut through and approached the summit from the other direction.

In order to gain the height required it appears French road builders threw the idea of a 10° maximum gradient out of the window, as the road slopes up at an alarming angle, for the second time in this trip I slipped into my 24t chain ring, once again I was going too slow to be stable, nor was it helped by the road, the mountain side of the road was still covered in packed snow/ice that was gradually receding. Between the road and the mountain side was a deep trench. As the ice had melted the shale behind it was slipping down the side and over the ditch and onto the road littering the surface with rocks from pea sized up to the size of footballs. Unable to dodge to the left for fear of heading into the ditch, swaying to the right could lead to a very quick descent, and being totally unstable at this speed I got off and pushed. It was fortunate that I did as moments later a car barely missed me at the side of the road as it too had to swerve to avoid a boulder that came tumbling down in front of us. Rounding the highest point of the road I parked the bike and admired the view of the mountain range stretching out below my feet.

Dominic had bet me by a good margin and had opted to climb the scree slope on foot to the very pinnacle of the mountain, but I was too tired to bother, also at this altitude the temperature had dropped, after rising to around 28° it was now once again in single figures and clouds were beginning to form over the surrounding peaks. Removing my jersey I rummaged through my panniers and added a long sleeved base layer and arm warmers before pulling on my gillet for the long descent. By this time Anne had joined us and explaining I wouldn't keep up on the descent as I would be constantly on the brakes Dominic told me of a café in Saint-Etienne-de-Tinee where they would wait over coffee. This was fine by me as this was my planned resting place for the night.

Despite hugging the inside of the road the descent from the Cime was a very fraught occupation, it would have been safer to get off and push in retrospect but once clear and onto the proper road the surface cleared up, I was once again on the outside edge but many of the corners had good sight lines and as my confidence built so did my speed. Soon the ground opens up through more grassland, while the gradient remains the offside does not feature massive mind numbing drops. Though I am sure coming off the road would be painful it would probably be survivable, and with this caution is cast pretty much to the wind.

Coming round a sharp bend both sides of the road open as the hillside drops away and the bizarre sight of a town street along the road comes into view. As I approach it is evident that like the barracks this too is completely abandoned, buildings are crammed together flanking both sides of the road but every one is completely derelict and roofless.

The valley walls once again start to come together and the road gets more perilous as I pass two small hamlets, the second has a small café with a table outside but no bikes in evidence, I continue not for one minute believing this could be our meeting point, besides the sat nav has not indicated that I have reached my destination. The road surface started to deteriorate and soon I was into resurfacing road works, slowing down to try and avoid punctures I once again marvelled at how the French managed to have perfectly smooth, unpotholed tarmac even when half the year it was under snow and ice, how they found the time and money to maintain roads to this extent that only serviced a few outlying communities and this without resorting to 'surface dressing'. Even where I had seen evidence of potholes they had been filled level with the surrounding surface and were unnoticeable travelling over them.

Soon I reached a larger town, realising it was my destination I looked around for a terraced café on the main road, nearly missing it as it was tucked away below the level of the road in the town square out of sight until I had drawn level. Sharply turning I spotted Dominic and Anne who were only too happy to order a second coffee and kindly buying mine as well.

Over coffee Dominic said that previously they had stayed at a glorious campsite with an exceptional Pizza café on site in Isola about 10km further down the road, and that rather than using the busy main road, if he could find it again, there was an excellent dedicated cycle path the entire distance. As I had to pass through Isola I said it would be a pleasure to join them for the evening.

After only one minor detour Dominic recognized the path we had to take and we set off in convoy to Isola. The campsite was a narrow strip bordered by the cycle path and the main road, the pizza café a wood hut with corrugated roof and bench tables, a small covered decked area outside looked out over an ornamental lake teeming with large fish. The campsite was virtually deserted and we were given free choice of pitch, the owner recognised Dominic and promised to open the restaurant for us despite the lack of clientele, and if we wanted any drinks to just shout.

No sooner had the tents gone up than the heavens opened and the rain started, fantastic timing for once, sat on the decking drinking a cold beer was a delight despite being huddled in jackets as the temperature had plummeted and the noise on the tin roof was drowning out conversation. Finally having a proper conversation I found that they had rented out their house out for the year and were travelling round on the bikes including England. Their most enjoyable time had been in Normandy and touring the battlefields around the Somme, Dominic was very animated about his findings including ammunition and armaments, they had even found human remains that had to be reported to the war office. He said they intended to cycle south to the coast before catching a train back

North and spending more time in the area. I explained my purpose for touring telling him of the plight of greyhounds and how this was my way of trying to raise a few pounds despite never having cycled seriously before, they immediately pledged to make a donation when they found internet access. Returning to my tent for a short nap before eating, Dominic called me over brandishing his bag of souvenirs, amongst the various bullets and bits of shrapnel he had an unexploded hand grenade, it must have been quite a unique piece and he was rightly proud of it. It was a British grenade with the pin still in now welded in place through corrosion, the unique thing was it was only half a grenade, it must have been blown to pieces by something else without actually exploding itself.

The pizza was everything that Anne had billed it to be, and the conversation was enjoyable as we exchanged tales from our travels. The rain continued as we bade goodnight and settled into our respective tents.

Day 7

The morning dawned overcast and drizzly, whether it was because there were two of them or if I was less enthusiastic about setting off, Dominic and Anne had their tent bagged and their bikes loaded before I had even finished my bowl of muesli, they were heading into Isola for their breakfast and we agreed to meet up at a café Dominic had visited on a previous trip.

Preparing for what looked like it was going to be a miserable day of cycling I dressed in arm and leg warmers, waterproof jacket and overshoes, it wasn't quite bad enough for waterproof trousers. The previous day the owner of the campsite could not be bothered opening the office so consequently before heading off I had to find her to pay not only for the camping but also the evenings meal and drinks, very trusting the French.

The camp site was located a kilometre or so from Isola and reaching the roundabout I tossed a mental coin whether to continue on or go meet Dominic, deciding that it was best to keep with our arrangement I headed uphill into the small town, not spotting their bikes, at first I headed into the first shop which turned out to be a mishmash of butchers and café, nothing really appealed, nor did the prices, but suddenly feeling quite peckish I opted for a slice of cheese on toast or croquet monsieur as it is called, despite it costing nearly 3 euros it was possibly the best cheese on toast I have ever eaten.

After wandering the street eating my early morning snack I spotted a couple of familiar looking bikes leant against a doorway so I popped inside to grab a coffee to wish my fellow travellers bon voyage as they headed south to the Med and I cut west for the long journey overland. As I walked through the door Anne jumped up and bought me a coffee, sitting down Dominic explained they had been talking and would like me to accept all the spare sterling they still had for my charity cycle ride and as it only amounted to about £12 could they have my email address so they could donate more when they returned home! What a lovely couple.

Setting off after a second cup of coffee we soon split up each cycling at their own speed, though it was downhill for once I found myself at the front. I knew the right hand junction I wanted was the first one off the road we were on and that it wasn't until the town of St-Sauveur. Looking on the road map this junction appeared to be in the town itself, after cycling at a reasonable speed along a road that was littered with fallen rocks for a few kilometres I spotted a right hand turn not where I expected and not looking particularly like the main road I had expected either, this road was at 180 ° and travelled over a very narrow bridge.

I checked the sat nav only to find the cable from the battery pack had once again come loose from the see-sawing descent from Isola, thinking it prudent to stop and at least reconnect the power I was quickly joined by my antipodean friends. The sat nav confirmed that this was indeed my turning so my stopping had been fortuitous and had allowed me to say a final farewell, though with the weather still slightly inclement it took a fair amount of willpower to turn down their offer of joining them towards Cannes!

The Col de La Couillole is 16km and climbs 1168m, the gradient is an average 7.5% and is fairly steady varying between 6 and 9%. There are no markers for cyclists offering the percentage but there are marker posts showing the distance to the next hamlet and town. After the first few corners the sun won the battle with the cloud and I was soon making the decision to strip off down to just shorts and jersey. As the road makes its way up the valley side darting through several short tunnels I caught my first glance of an impossibly perched town stead near the summit of the towering mountain. Hoping vainly that my route didn't involve reaching this place! Of course it did and after a surprisingly short time I came across a series of sharp hairpins that led into this small commune that was more of a ski station than the village I had perceived it to be. The signpost informing me that I was still 5 km from the Col.

Despite the chalets appearing to be at the summit this was a false impression as rounding this peak gave way to the full splendour of the mountain range in front. Continuing I passed a farmstead with various childs toys littering the edge of the road, a little further on I spotted a bright green and red plastic/rubber bendy lizard in the middle of the road, thinking that some poor child was about to get his toy destroyed by the next passing car I prepared to stop and retrieve it. Just as I was pulling to a halt the 'toy' scurried to the road side and under a boulder. Darn wish I had a camera handy, but at the time it gave me quite a start.

After passing the Col de La Couillole, and a short descent I arrived at the small town of Beuil. By now the temperature had risen from 10° to a rather warm 34° and the exertion of the climb had taken its toll on my energy and liquid resources. In Beuil there was a choice of eateries but opting for one set back from the road with plenty of outside tables with parasols seemed like a good idea. I enjoyed a very large and tasty salad whilst keeping the Madame busy replenishing the iced water carafe!

According to all sources there was a campsite in Puget-Theniers so I opted to descend via the Gorges du Cians. The gorge road descends 1600m over 25km and should be a fast twisty fun descent, or so the theory went. The walls of the Gorge are red rock and offer an impressive sight, the gorge itself is about 80m deep with a raging torrent at its base. The walls of the canyon are unstable and the road workers have nailed wire mesh on the steeper sections in an attempt to contain rock slides but soon into the ride it becomes evident that whilst it may help motorised traffic the amount of small pebbles and flint like rocks scattering the road are not conducive to fast flowing cycling!

As the road heads downwards toward the river it cuts through numerous short tunnel sections that have been bored through the rock in particularly unstable areas, the old road still evident but cordoned off to large vehicles around the outside. I decided on one particularly long section to try the outer route, but as this had not been cleared for a long period so I had to dismount and push, the road was damaged beyond repair and when it had been open must have been treacherous in areas barely more than a car width wide.

At about the halfway point down the gorge it narrows, the river is barely a few meters wide and the road seems to be touching the far wall with rocky overhangs virtually doing so giving the impression of further tunnels. This of course means the road is covered in even more debris especially at the edge of the road, and it became a nerve wracking experience trying to negotiate the bends whilst avoiding rocks and cars full of sightseers travelling in both directions. Once again the French idea of road safety is a barrier at the side of the road towering a heady 18" in height.

Whilst in the shadow of the canyon walls at least the temperature dropped to a more manageable 23° though as soon as I exited and out on to the main road to Puget this increased to an even higher 37° and of course the highly populated main carriageway is on a constant uphill gradient of around 2%.

My sat nav was programmed to take me straight to the camp ground, which turned out to be the grounds of a hospital and a public park, adjacent to a set of tennis courts. Unsure where to pitch up I searched for signs of a concierge or failing that a public lavatory that would allow me my ablutions if I just pitched up in the park. Having no such luck I headed back into the town to ask.

Luckily almost as soon as I reached the main road I spotted a sign for a tourist information centre. The lady inside fortunately spoke reasonable English and with my broken French I was able to piece together that the campsite was indeed where I had been, but had been closed down the previous year. She told me the name of the next campsite and said it was about 5 minutes away. Now if the Spanish are famed for how far they can oik a stone to the sea, then the French must be in the same league as to how far they can travel in 5 minutes!

Searching for the campsite on the sat nav it turned out to be 10km down the main road, this was possibly the most unenjoyable part of my trip to date, I began to dream of the cooling rain! The main road was wind swept, the heat didn't let up, the traffic was horrendous and the entire journey soulless, for the icing on the cake after a short while I was busting for a pee without a single bush in sight.

After cycling a while I came across the walled town of Entravaux which the lady in the information centre had mentioned as the point I should join the cycle path. The old walled town is situated over a river and accessed by bridge, seeing no signs for a cycle way I continued to follow my sat nav along the main road. This road follows a wide flood plain with what look like half-finished bridges protruding from the adjacent hillside, these carry flood waters over the road and pour straight onto the flood plain.

After cycling for another 30 minutes I came across a sign advertising the campsite, this was a sharp 180° junction off to the right. The road carried on back in the direction of Entravaux but on the other side of the flood plain, eventually ending in a large campsite with a Leisure Lake.

Booking in for the night I discovered that the camp was owned and run by a British family and the road did continue back into Entravaux so no doubt had my French been better I could have saved a few miles of cycling. As soon as the tent was up and the bike secured I thought it would be nice to cool off with a swim in the lake. Moored in the centre of the lake was a pontoon for sunbathing/diving. The mooring ropes, unbeknown to me stretched out at quite an angle and shortly after swimming out into the lake the first sensation I had was of something thick, long, and slimy brushing against my leg. Thinking I was about to get eaten by a prehistoric French eel it wasn't until I noticed a rope snaking out of the water at the bank opposite the pontoon I realised what had happened.

Calming my nerves with a well-deserved bottle of beer in the campsite café I decided that I wanted something more substantial than the sausage and chips on offer and that a walk into town was in order. After a shower and a change I set out along the road to Entravaux, this soon turned into rock strewn trail and I was relieved that I hadn't found it earlier and tried to cycle it. The walk took about 30 minutes before I found myself climbing a steep stone stair mounting the battlements of the towns' wall.

There is only one way to describe the town and that is quaint, I would imagine that during the day the place would be a hive of activity but as it was all the artisans were boarded up and only the main square housing its restaurants was coming to life. I enjoyed a long leisurely evening meal washed down with beer and wine before stumbling my way back to camp along the unlit rocky path, though the return trip did seem quicker than the way there!

Day 8

The day started nice and a cool 12°, but the sun was already out and there wasn't a cloud in the sky. Breakfast was the last of my muesli and whey powder mix that had made it from the UK, after this the only 'food' I had left were three energy gels which aren't exactly appetizing.

Today I was aiming to reach the Verdon Gorge and expected to reach Castellane in time for lunch. The main N road from Entrevaux to Ste-Julien-du-Verdon climbs at a steady 4% all the way to the top of the Col de Toutes Aures before dropping towards the Lac de Castillon where I intended to join a smaller D road that runs the length of the lake and into Castellane.

The first part of the journey along the N202 was a fraught affair, the road surface was reasonable and the view excellent as I made my way up and along the valley side, unfortunately the traffic whilst not particularly heavy was consistent. I was worried then when I came across traffic light controlled road works that looped off into the distance and could be seen to continue along the valley side as the road snaked its way along. The section of road left for traffic was barely wide enough for one of the large quarry lorries that had been steadily approaching me all morning, let alone wide enough if I was caught in the middle of the road works after the lights had changed. Fortunately as I neared the lights they changed to red meaning I would at least be at the front of the queue and have the most time to navigate the obstruction. Not so fortunate for the traffic building up behind as there wasn't room for them to pass once in the road works, and on a 4% slope I wasn't going to be moving fast!

The road works continued for a good 1500m and as it was Sunday there was no actual work taking place, this meant I was able to cycle in the cordoned off area and let traffic past and have somewhere to hide if the lights changed, which of course they did, cycling with only a meter and a line of cones between myself and oncoming 20 ton lorries was no fun at all.

A short while later and with the temperature now in the twenties I spotted a small hotel nestled in the crook of a bend at a junction and decided I deserved a morning coffee and cake. Having recently seen one of the 'Transporter' films I thought it would be nice to try fresh baked Madelaines, but of course being Sunday the chef wasn't working and the only Madelaines on offer where commercial foil wrapped affairs, still tasty but a complete rip off.

The descent from the Col was a welcome respite from the 20+km of steady climb and the cobalt blue waters of the lake looked heavenly for a swim in the now 28° heat. Not seeing anywhere where swimming looked sensible or allowed I continued on my way to Castellane.

I arrived in Castellane at around 11am, too early for lunch, and the place was packed with what I presumed were tourists. The biggest disadvantage of cycle touring is what do you do with a bike that has all your goods and chattels strapped to it. On a campsite I felt quite safe leaving my pannier bags in the tent and the bike chained to a tree, but in the middle of a bustling town I didn't fancy leaving the whole lot fastened to a set of railings with nothing to stop my panniers or tent from going walkies. So much as I would have liked to explore Castellane and buy food in one of the many boulangeries that were actually open I opted to continue on my way and find a café or restaurant on the outskirts.

Heading towards the Verdon Gorge the only eatery I passed didn't look very appetising and as I was still early I decided to push on and have lunch at a pizzeria on the way to Trigance that I had already earmarked for that evening when planning my camping place.

After following the river Verdon I followed the river-a-gauche sign and headed up hill towards Soleils and found a lovely quiet restaurant/pizzeria cut into the hillside with the most dramatic view over the escarpments of the Verdon Gorge. I was still too early for lunchtime service and all the staff were sat around the terrace enjoying an aperitif before work (what a sensible idea), taking pity on me with the temperature now up into the thirties I was offered a Pastis and multiple bottles of iced water. The pizza equalled any I have ever had, the only downside was sharing it with the local wildlife as a variety of flying creatures kept descending on my position, the final nail was the appearance of a large lizard scurrying under my table before perching itself on the rock wall adjacent to my head, fortunately all it did was bask in the sun.

My original plan had been to camp at the large commercial site at the entry to the Verdon Gorge, but as it was still only midday I decided to push on, I had two choices, to continue on the left of the river which was a longer steeper more undulating route to Moustiers that followed the course of the river along the Corniche Sublime, or alternatively, to drop back down to where I had crossed the river and climb the escarpment riding through the forested areas before dropping back onto the rivers course and entering Moustiers, this route still involved a lot of climbing but was less undulating.

 I opted for the 'easy' option and headed downhill back to the river to follow it until it veered off at the Point Sublime and I headed uphill. By now the afternoon sun was a blast furnace and my thermometer was reading 41°. I was more than happy to abandon plans to reach Moustiers and make do with making only ½ a day so when a municipal campsite came into view on the outskirts of La Palud-sur-Verdon I was only too happy to stop.

At first the campsite looked closed apart from a couple of camper vans (who park anywhere in any case) but on closer examination a notice in the office window said the place was only manned for 2 hours a day at 3pm to 5pm and to set up and pay then. I pitched my tent in the shade of the biggest tree I could find and stripped off inside to try and cool down, read a book and rest. Waking up an hour or so later drenched with sweat from contact with the plastic bed mat I headed off for a shower and to get dressed in something other than lycra. A quick shower and I was ready to check out the town for my evening entertainment, the office was open so I paid my pittance of a fee and set off up the road, whilst the temperature had not dropped and it was still in the forties it was more comfortable walking than lying. The town was nothing more than a church square and a couple of streets, the road I was on continued straight through, the alternative led along a tortuous but scenic loop back to the edge of the escarpment and along the river, one I would have liked to try on the bike but not today!

My choices for the evening were a creperie that appeared to closed with no intentions of opening, a gaudy bar/café, a pizza van parked up in a layby or a small Spa shop. Though the Pizza van appeared to be doing a good trade it didn't particularly appeal so I went to the Spa shop and bought the components for an evening picnic. Four bottles of beer, a baguette, tomatoes, butter, ham, a brie and a bar of chocolate. In total it probably cost more than any meal I had eaten so far, it shocked me how much a couple of slices of pre-packed meat cost in France.

Returning to the campsite I set down to enjoy my repast saving half the bread and cheese for breakfast. Using the toilet block for my evening ablution I could only find a traditional hole in the floor toilet and the disabled toilet was locked so I vowed in the following morning I would have to call into the café for a coffee and to use their 'hopefully' more western facilities, it surprised me being so far south how quickly and early the sun sets and how complete the night is, the kindle had to be put away and I was quickly asleep.

Day 9

Today proved to be my stupidest decision yet. Having made half a day yesterday I had the choice of a very easy 50km or a mind numbing 133km. Not realising the latter option was quite so bad at the time or that it involved climbing 1902m I opted to make up a full day, giving me 2 days in hand over my original schedule. There was some logic to this, if the weather was particularly windy the following day for my trip over Ventoux I could just take a day of rest.

The day started cool, waking up at 6.30am the temperature was a chilly 9° after the previous days low forties. Quickly packing away I set off up the hill to call in for an early morning pit stop at the towns café, luckily it was open and the facilities weren't a 'Turkish' toilet and even had soft loo roll, well worth paying £2 for a cup of coffee.

I was soon descending back toward the gorge floor with magnificent views of the Verdon river crashing its way along its rock strewn path. Rounding one corner the gorge opened up and the spectacle of the expanse of the Lac de Sainte Croix spread off to my left several hundred feet below. Leaving the Verdon Gorge behind I skirted the town of Moustiers and continued on the main road to Riez where I would turn off for my overnight stop of Valensole. I had been hoping for a room in for Valensole using the 'Couchsurfing' website but it had fallen through when the host had changed jobs and moved, he had however provided details of what he described as an brilliant campsite. By the time I had reached Riez the temperature had reached the high twenties and with plenty of time in hand I stopped at the first pavement café with a railing to lean the bike against. After a very pleasurable ½ hour watching the world go by I set off on the undulating road to Valensole.

Arriving in Valensole before 11am I made the decision to push on to Sault and make a further ½ day, so far I had covered only 48km with 580m of height gain. I was now once again cycling through fields of wheat or barley and along the Ravin de Vallongue which led to an interesting race with a local tractor who must have had a limited top speed of around 40kmh as I was flying past him on the steeper downhill stretches only to have him pull slowly round me every time the route flattened out.

At the foot of the climb is the city of Manosque, blindly following the sat nav I was led the wrong way down a one way street that was in the middle of road works. From what I could gather from the signage the one way system was only just being introduced and the road was closed for the works to alter signs and put traffic calming measures in place, dismounting and pushing I decided it was easier to plead ignorance than find an alternative route, fortunately I avoided officialdom.

The road I took out of Manosque started straight up the Col de Montfuron at only 649m this shouldn't have been any great issue but the temperature was now up at 39° and I was glad of the 3 litres of fluid I was carrying in my backpack even if it was now luke warm.

At the foot of the following descent I came across a single story prefab building set back from the road and lit up with fairy lights, the signage informed me that it was pizzeria, so that was a leisurely lunch sorted, and very nice it was, I also took the opportunity to top up my water bladder as well as drinking a good litre of ice cold water with a very agreeable pizza.

I thought I was cycling through France with a great history of gastronomy and fantastic local dishes, served cheaply in out of way small towns for the local farmers to enjoy their 3 hour lunch breaks, but instead everywhere was Pizza. I like Pizza but it was getting a bit repetitive, I wanted to find French food and all the French seem to eat is Pizza these days. Maybe I had taken too much notice of 'A Year in Provence', and was expecting too much.

After lunch which took me up to about 2pm things started to go downhill whilst still travelling uphill. I had about 50km to cover and a thousand meters of climbing before reaching Sault and the sun in the mid afternoon was showing no respite. The crops along the road started to change, all the fields where a carpet of purple and the scent of lavender hung heavy in the air, in the distance from the top of the hills I could just about make out what appeared to be the summit of

Ventoux giving me false hope of the time it would take me. Whilst sat nav had not been the most reliable piece of technology I had ever used, apart from the odd one way street so far it hadn't sent me far wrong. This afternoon was to prove the exception, the road started to deteriorate and then turned into a track, it was probably a road years ago but now it was impassable, even on foot it didn't look promising.

My sat nav has a function that allows you to ask for an alternative route in case of a road block, unfortunately it appeared that its mapping not only includes roads but also footpaths or bridleways, after an extremely frustrating toeing and froing as the sat nav continually tried to put me at different points along the now non-existent road I opted to ignore its instruction altogether and examine the map to try and find road that would eventually take me to a place I wanted to be. I finally devised my own alternative route that would take me into the town of Simiane-la-Rotonde.

It was not however to be plain sailing, the temperature had now reached 42° and my water bladder was getting unnervingly light on my back despite having already re-filled it once. Starting to feel rather light-headed and altogether downhearted I was starting to worry about sunstroke and de-hydration. Since eating there had been no civilisation whatsoever not even a farm building on the road side. It was with a great amount of relief that in the distance I spotted a large low building with a walled garden and the most glorious looking swimming pool. Thinking even if it was a deserted holiday home for the rich I would take advantage of an illicit swim if nothing else, and powered on towards my new goal.

It was in fact a Luxury boutique Chamber des Hautes according to the sign, riding into the gravelled courtyard there was no one about and it wasn't until I had ventured around the building into the garden that I came across a giant of a man relaxing on a sun lounger. Trying to converse in French that I would very much like a room he quickly interrupted me in fluent English saying he was a friend of the Dutch owners and was managing the place for the summer and that he was very sorry but all the rooms were taken. He did offer the use of the swimming pool if I did want a dip, but the thought of having to get straight back on the bike put me off, not lest as time was getting on. I did say that water would be most acceptable and instead of taking me to the nearest tap he came out with a liter bottle of iced liquid straight from the fridge, I am not sure he was expecting me to pour it into my backpack but he was very sporting and brought me a further 2 bottles out.

Having had my thirst quenched and feeling a little better for the 20 minutes out of the saddle I set off down the road from the villa at a fair turn of speed. I don't know if French bees all fly backwards but the pain I felt when one hit me on the forehead was intense, reaching up to see what on earth had hit me I had the rather shocking task of removing the bee from my skin by its body and having to pull its sting out, This was the first time in 43 years that I had ever been stung by a bee, and being paranoid to start with for the next quarter of an hour all I could think about was whether I would go into anaphylactic shock or not, I could truly appreciate why cyclist always wear glasses!

Having rejoined the route depicted by sat nav I reached Simiane-la-Rotonde, after a much longer ride than expected. Saint-Christol the next town on my route and sits on a mound at the foot of a hillside with the approach through flat farmland, looking very imposing it was obviously fortified in its early days. Cycling around its base and into the hills beyond I start passing the pale stone houses I have imagined this area of France to be populated by, none appear to be habituated and get the impression many are holiday homes.

After 133km and with the time approaching 6pm I finally cycle into Sault, and find a welcome water fountain outside the tourism office. Enquiring within I find that the nearest campsite is a few kilometres out of town, the alternative being a B&B in the town centre at £50 a night. Worried as much about my bike in town as the price I follow the direction and set out for the campsite, at least the route is flat.

The campsite in Sault is located in a wooded area and is massive, on this occasion it was packed with some sort of school or scout gathering leaving me worried they wouldn't have space. Luckily they managed to squeeze me in. The swimming pool however was an extra and was in any case full of screaming kids. After a well deserve shower I wandered over to the reception building to find out about food, they were just closing the office and one of the staff offered to give me a lift back into Sault so I could find a proper restaurant, despite the fact he lived nowhere near the centre of town after hearing of my travels he insisted on driving me into the heart of Sault before wishing me good night and good luck with my future travels, top man, but I have to say your car is a death trap!

I was aching and tired and didn't fancy scouring the town to try and find the best place to eat, starting from the 'gardens' opposite the tourist information I did however quickly rule out the ubiquitous Pizza van. Walking into town I came across a hotel with a courtyard restaurant advertising a 15E 22E and 30E menu, throwing caution to the wind I went in, sat down and asked for a menu. Deciding I was worth it after my daily exertions I decided on the 30Emenu that consisted of 7 courses, none of them pizza and all typical French cuisine. Washed down with a couple of large beers and a bottle of red wine I was well and truly stuffed for the long walk back to the campsite without any kind Samaritan to give me a lift. This was now my best meal of the holiday so far.

Day 10

Again the day dawned beautiful and clear with no wind, so I decided to take advantage and was off and running by 7am for my assault on the 'easy' side of Mt. Ventoux. Reaching Sault 10 minutes later I stopped to purchase a breakfast of pain au chocolate and a cake thing that looked interesting for later in the ride, the patisserie on the edge of the small square was how I would have imagined a traditional French cake shop to look with hundreds of wooden shelves all laden down with exciting fresh baked confectionery.

The sign post for Ventoux out of Sault points down a narrow street leading onto a sharp downhill, these few hundred yards of freewheeling are the last for 26km. The road crosses a small bridge winding gradually uphill through the lavender fields before reaching the treeline. For today I was wearing a new pair of shorts that I had not used before and it wasn't far into the trees that I became aware that they were beginning to chafe. Pulling to a stop I must have looked a fair old sight as I rearranged my gentlemen's veg and slapped on large dollops of ass lard! The surface of the road from Sault was quite broken up and the ride up to Chalet Reynard wasn't entirely pleasurable.

At the Chalet they were only just opening up and I was the first customer of the day, taking a seat outside on the apex of the corner to watch fellow cyclists suffering I sat back and enjoyed a coffee and the cake I had carried from Sault.

For my journey my wife had made me a couple of mascots, a small and a larger stuffed greyhound, one standing round 4" the other 6" the smaller had been the prototype and I had decided I wanted to leave it at the shrine of British Tour de France rider Tom Simpson who died whist racing up this mountain. The shrine stands a little over a kilometre from the summit and is strewn with riders offerings from gloves to water bottles. From Sault the first 22k to Chalet Reynard is relatively easy at an average gradient of less than 6%, the next 6 ½ km average over 8%. I was glad to stop at the memorial and spend a few minutes paying my respects.

The final couple of hairpins harbour gradients of around 10% with the final short ramp onto the summit being a leg straining 15%+, whilst feeling a little fresher after the stop at the Chalet and at Tom's memorial I was apprehensive when I was chased down once again by a photographer proffering a card with the time and date stamped on telling me the website to visit to order my photos, this was third occasion in 1km!! By the time I had reached the summit and abandoned my bike for a photo the temperature had risen from 9° to 27° making my decision to set off early a sensible one.

At the summit there was a group of young lads that I had watched cycle past whilst having my coffee at the Chalet, now collapsed over their carbon fibre racing bikes, hearing them speak English I asked if they would mind taking a photo of myself with the bike. I think he was rather demoralised when he saw that a portly old bloke had cycled up the same hill as himself whilst carrying a 30kg load on a 15kg bike, and he was the one gasping for breath and still waiting for some of his party to catch up!! Having talked a while and told him the route I had already cycled, (ok so I was bragging) he said they had been in the area a few days and today they were attempting 'les Cingles' * This was their first climb of the day, wishing them luck, privately I didn't fancy their chances. There are a couple of souvenir shops selling commemorative jerseys and overpriced coke under the weather station that sits atop Ventoux and in this widened area at the peak there were also several market barrows selling a variety of items from sweets to hot dogs (and probably pizza!!) What stood out as strange to me standing on top of this iconic mountain was the stalls selling cheese and another selling sausage, who would travel all this way to by a slab of cheese or a kilo of gourmet sausage?

The descent of Ventoux into Malaucene was glorious, probably the steepest side of the mountain but without too many hairpins, a wide road and well surfaced, I soon found my confidence to lean even my loaded tourer into the bends and keep the momentum flying rather than hanging on the brakes the entire way down. Malaucene was packed with bikes and cyclists and seeing '000's of pounds worth of machinery left against the trees and railings I decided my bike and kit would be quite safe.

As I walked round it was evident that every café table was taken, the lads I had spoken to earlier were perched on the steps of a local store eating vacuum packed sandwiches, which didn't really appeal to me. Rather than continue on my journey I started looking at the restaurants that would be opening shortly and found a promising looking spot offering a three course plate de jour for 10E, it didn't open for a good half hour so I opted to spend the time looking at bike porn in the local bike shop.

For the money the meal was good but nothing to remember, other than at least it wasn't pizza, I was looking forward to what I hoped would be something special for my evening treat as I was heading for Chateauncuf de Pape and expected the town to be full of restaurants offering gourmet food quaffed down by excellent local vintage wine, the main reason the town was on my route.

The ride from Malaucene was 35km and though not particularly hilly it was undulating and with the temperature once again reaching 40° I was ready for a rest. I knew I was nearing my destination as the lavender fields gave way to acre after acre of vines, and I was relieved to reach the town of Chateauneuf de Pape. The campsite which I had been warned about for its midge problem was situated a mile or so from the town and adjacent to a river. Upon arrival after some chasing round trying to find someone in the office I was given a choice of three pitches, picking the flattest I started to pitch my tent only to have a family roll up a few minutes later and start to do the same on the same pitch. After a mild misunderstanding it turned out that they had seen a different member of staff and been told that this was their pitch, rather than argue I opted to move on to the next area, not as flat but it was only for one night. Once again the swimming pool was an extra and was in anycase particularly small and busy, so I opted for a long afternoon siesta before a welcome shower and a walk into town.

At the best of times I am a midge magnet, which is why for this trip I was taking anti bite tablets, and had anti midge patches, despite this I woke from my siesta with several red lumps as evidence of the little blighters appetite, and the shower was a welcome relief. The walk into town showed further evidence of its fame as a wine producer, passing several bottling plants with literally hundreds of thousands of empty bottles stacked in their yards waiting for filling. Reaching town I settled on a bench in the small square to enjoy a little bit of shade whilst drinking an ice cold drink from the local Spa shop, and waiting for the restaurants to open for evening service.

Wandering around the town which was surprisingly small I was struggling to find a restaurant, there were dozens of wine caves offering tastings and bargains on cases of wine but given I was already loaded down and on a bike they weren't of much use, I finally found a restaurant and was disappointed that the menu didn't include the local wine. In fact the entire town let alone the meal was a disappointment, maybe I had built it up in my mind and was expecting too much, or I just hadn't discovered the right place, either way I was soon walking back to camp for a well deserved nights sleep.

Tonight was the first night I noticed the French crickets, the noise they make at night is deafening and I was laid in my sleeping bag thinking I would never get to sleep. But one minute there was a racket the next complete silence, not so much as a chirp.

*Les Cingles, a select group of cyclists who have managed to climb Mt. Ventoux via all three
routes in one day.

Day 11

Another glorious day dawned and with no provisions to hand a quick wash and de-camp soon had me cycling back to the town for my onward journey. Not relishing a plastic packed sandwich from the local mini mart, and having not seen a boulangerie the previous evening I opted to continue straight on to my 'tourist' destination of the day 'Pont-du-Gard' and stop anywhere on route that took my fancy. After cycling through what I can only describe as some surreal landscape, like a manmade attraction of dotted small hills and brushland I found myself on a more populated road with a boulangerie, woohhoo. With the time around 9.30am and with another hour or so to go to my first destination I stopped to buy both breakfast and lunch on the basis that I expected anything on sale at Pont-du-Gard would be ridiculously overpriced. A slice of quiche lorraine, a jumbo sausage roll, and a couple of pain au chocolat for about 5 E I deemed to be a bargain and munched down on the choccy delicacy for brekky. Yummy, if the rest of my purchases where of equal quality then I suspected I should have bought more!!

It was not much further on that I surprisingly came across some of the steepest hills on my ride to date, or as we know them, sleeping Gendarmes, and it was the jolting of one of these that had at some point caused the daily disconnection of the sat nav from the battery pack. Of course the darned thing decided to let me know this had occurred by switching itself off on a steep uphill on a moderately busy road through town approaching a roundabout, sods law.

A roman aqueduct thingy in the middle of nowhere or the 'Nord-du-Gard' if you prefer is pretty spectacular when viewed in pictures, in real life it is even better, however like all tourist attractions the surrounding area as been spoilt by the infrastructure required to accommodate the number of visitors it attracts. What was probably once a rural back road now widens into a dual carriageway that ends in a massive series of car parks more akin to Birminghams NEC then a feat of Roman engineering masterpiece. Arriving by bike I was left slightly dazed by the route I had to take to enter the park grounds that surround the 'bridge'. It was also beyond my meagre language capabilities to work out if I was expected to pay, in the end I deciphered that entry was free and you were meant to pay for parking. Entry into the park is through a rather grand pedestrian precinct/mall type structure, and discretion being the better part of valour I thought it best to dismount and walk.

Once inside the 'grounds' there are a plethora of paths to explore with lots of plants and wildlife to admire along the way, the paths are relatively wide and whilst driving is banned other people were cycling so I decided it was ok providing speed was kept low, I opted to take the quickest and shortest route to the main attraction. Surprisingly pedestrians (and cyclists) are still allowed to walk (ride) on the structure so accessing the far side of the river was easy and taking the opportunity of a little bit of shade I opted to have an early lunch, both the sausage roll and quiche lived up to the earlier promise and I did give passing thought to retracing my steps and returning for more, however a two hour return journey made it a very fleeting thought! Returning over this ancient structure I did have to wonder how long it would be before some do-gooder/ conservationist decided to rope it off and only allow tourists to look at it from a safe distance whilst paying through the nose for the privilege, thank goodness it isn't in England!

Having spent enough time looking and taking pictures, (I came, I saw, I buggered off, I am not a person to dilly dally) and deciding whilst appealing in the heat, it would be too much trouble to descend to the foot of the gorge, strip off and go for a swim, I set off for the long slog to the town of Sommieres.

Shortly after mid-day passing through the town of Collias I checked the sat nav and discovered I still had a demoralising 48km to cycle to my destination, having a couple of days in hand before needing to be in place to catch the Tour de France, I made the very easy decision to back track the kilometer or so to what had appeared to be a very attractive camp site. Expecting to have to pay through the nose when I arrived (the site had electric barriers and was obviously much better appointed than I was used to) the night price of 8E was a very pleasant surprise, and they had a plot free, just the one, and only when its current incumbents had departed, but a stroke of luck none the less.

The couple vacating the pitch had just finished packing as I cycled up so wasting no time I had the tent pitched in double quick time and the speedos on ready for a dip in the camp pool. Not before the couple had returned looking for a lost pair of sunglasses. (Never did find them, sorry)

The pool was invitingly cool and a welcome change of exercise to pedalling, it being a very popular site though meant the pool was also busy, mainly with children, so any chance of muscle relaxing length swimming was pretty much out of the equation, 20 minutes did the job of cooling me down and it was time for a swift beer at the poolside bar followed by a shower. I had now been cycling for 9 days without washing any clothes, not quite pheweee but everything had been worn twice, adjacent to the shower block was a laundry room and with it only being 2.30pm and hot, hot, hot the time had come to find some washing powder. Returning to the tent to grab my washing I heard English voices in the touring caravan next door, never one to be backward in coming forward asking my neighbours if they had any washing powder seemed the easiest (and cheapest) option. The young lady was kind enough to offer me two varieties, a tube of gunk or a box of powder, so thinking that I hoped her parents didn't mind off I toddled to wash and rinse my smalls. (I did consider asking if she fancied doing it for me but that might have been pushing my luck).

After returning (what was left) the washing aids and bodging up a washing line from tree to tent (it was a bodge as well as I had left my spare guy rope in Sault) it was time to explore the local town and suss if an eatery for the evening meal was available and better than the camp cafe offering (the cafe on the camp as opposed to a cafe doing a Dale Winton impression). The main action in the town appeared to be on the riverbank with various cafes and concession kiosks meeting the need of the tourism high spot of kayaking on the river, none of which however filled my need to find a decent evening meal. Even when I am touring on a bike I like to eat well and enjoy going out on an evening for a proper sit down meal, and if that is authentic to the region, even better. The rest of the town was small but had a very pretty church and church square, off of which I found the only restaurant. Even with my desire to eat well I could neither afford nor thoil the prices, the cheapest menu on the list was 220E and the dearest 400E and no that isn't a typing error, 9 courses and the price difference appeared to down to the selection of glass of wine that was served with each course. Oh to be rich.

Back at the campsite and after a quick pre-evening snooze, siding of the washing it was off to the camp cafe for a beer or three and to sample the offering. To be fair I played it relatively safe with veal and pomme frites and it was actually very enjoyable and cheap. Watching the lady on the next table get her mussels and frites which came in a mixing bowl (there must have been hundreds of the buggers) I thought sod it, an extra day relaxing here might be in order, swimming pool, and a chance to try kayaking, why not? Bloody Chav Frenchman that's why not!!

Returning to my tent to read before turning in for the night I noticed my neighbours in their awning attacking the vino and thought I could be in for a noisy night and would be making use of the earplugs. I was not wrong but soon found out the conversation was much more interesting than any novel could be. The young lady who had kindly loaned me the washing paraphernalia was actually holidaying with her school friend at the end of their exams. From what I could gather the pair of them had been left there for a fortnight by her parents who would be returning at the weekend to pick them up. As the wine flowed next door so did the conversation. It sounded like the elder of the two (whose parents caravan it was) had a bad experience with her last boyfriend and had decided to experiment and to turn to the dark side (being honest it was one hell of a waste as neither of them had exactly been hit with the ugly stick). Anyway she was doing everything and saying everything she could think of to get into her friends knickers, from professing undying love, to begging, to slagging off the male species. I never found out if she succeeded but before I finally fell asleep to enjoyable dreams I did work out that the friend wasn't completely averse but had found the use of tongues when kissing her a weird experience and being a good catholic had yet to try, and wanted to try a man before making up her mind, maybe she decided to try the furry cup first before making a comparison? Had I not been married, over 40 and knackered maybe I would have gone round and offered my services purely on scientific grounds.

Tomorrow was going to be interesting, if I bumped into them would it be fair to let them know how much sound travels at night and through canvas walls of a caravan awning? Would it be more embarrassing for them to be told? Could anybody else on the campsite within earshot understand English? (it was predominantly populated by French families) Despite the earplugs the sound of a dog barking woke me with a jolt, this was then proceeded (and from the sounds of it preceded) by a loud exchange in French between a inebriated French yob and the rest of his pig ignorant family. I don't like being woken up, or being kept awake for that matter when I am tired, as many a Scout that as ever been camping with me will testify and after checking my watch (1am) and putting up with the racket for a good 20 minutes I lost my rag and shouted at the top of my voice for the child to go to sleep and for the father to shut the f*** up, in my best Franglais. This was probably not the most diplomatic thing I have ever done, but in my defence I have done exactly the same thing on English campsites (and out of my bedroom window when next doors where getting on my tits for that matter) though obviously not in Franglais, anyway it elicited a tacit response (F&*^ off home you English W^%$£$£) from the recipient, another said (I think) well said Anglaise, and of course woke anyone who was still asleep. At least silence resumed shortly after, even the dog was quiet. It did mean of course that discretion etc etc meant I wouldn't be taking the day off on the 'morrow, and I would never find out if my neighbour had been successful in taking her friend to the dream Isle of Lesbos.

Day 12

Having not had what could be called a good nights sleep I awoke early and after a quick wash and brush up was ready to exit the campsite by 7am. My final act was to fill my water bladder, unfortunately the tap was exceedingly noisy and woke a dog in a tent adjacent to its location, hearing a string of expletives aimed at the hound I realised it was the resting place of mon ami from (much) earlier in the morning, karma.

The lack of breakfast and sleep, combined with the fact that I had promised myself a rest day meant I quickly made the decision to have a short day and only cycle as far as Sommieres, the town I had originally meant to reach the previous afternoon and only a couple of hours away at 46 km. At least starting out early meant that the heat of the day had yet to make its appearance, the ubiquitous green flashing cross on a local chemist shop informing me it was a cool 12º.

From my exploration the previous afternoon I knew it would be a pointless task trying to find a boulangerie and the one general store/shack I had come across did not fill me with confidence of getting a tasty breakfast treat and so it wasn't until I was 5 km down the road at the town of Sanilhac that I saw the promising sign of a patisserie, there was even a bench on the roadside opposite. A lidded paper cup of coffee, croissant and slice of pizza left me very little change from the proffered 10 E note, and then failed to meet expectations, which were probably too high after the previous days delicious treats, none the less it had filled a hole and with the morning sun raising the temperatures I pressed on in good spirit.

The campsite I had targeted in Sommieres appeared on google earth to be located very close to town and on the edge of a large car park, there did not appear to be a pool and so it didn't appear to have much going for it, it had also been a pain to find any reference to it on the internet, following a very similar pattern to the site in Puget that no longer existed. Coupled with the apprehension of leaving my transport and belongings lying about in such a location, on arrival in

Sommieres I made the decision to locate another venue for the nights stay.

The use of sat nav is truly marvellous, not only does this 4" by 2" little plastic block have every road in Europe, every cycle path and track mapped in, it also as the location of every campsite. Although in the wrong direction for my travels the closest alternative was only a couple of k down the road affording me easy access to the town for an evening meal and afternoon explore, and having cycled through Sommieres it appeared to be quite a large and vibrant place that would be interesting to spend a few hours walking round in tourist mode. The campsite it led me to was definitely 5 star and then some, from the large flower bordered drive to the electric gates everything screamed luxury, not least of all the sight of a swimming pool in the grounds more akin to a water park with slides and flumes. Even so the advertised prices on the tariff board outside did look rather, to put it politely, unbelievable, surely they were referring to a family of four in an oversized caravan with electric hook up, staying for a week and not to some poor cyclist with a tent $2m^2$?

I am sure the receptionist was moonlighting from a Doctors surgery somewhere, having all the warmth and charm of a November evening on Ilkley Moor, admittedly I was standing resplendent in lycra gently dripping on the plush carpet (the temperature was now a balmy $28°$ and the campsite at the top of a hill) I was probably not their usual clientele. After what seemed like an eternity she kindly informed me that whilst they were incredibly busy she would be able to allocate me a space as I had explained my tent was tres petite, however she could not make any concession for this, or the fact I had arrived by bike and that I needed to pay the full amount in advance for my nights stay, that would be 42 E please. Coughing and spluttering I made as dignified an exit as I could with the thought that I must have stumbled upon the dearest campsite that France, if not Europe, had to offer.

The next campsite on the list provided by Bryton (my sat nav) was a further 3 km from Sommieres so meant that I would be forfeiting the afternoon and evenings exploration but as it was still only 11am I thought it worth checking out. In the middle of nowhere Camping-les-Chenes offered level shaded pitches, a swimming pool and camp shop for 8E per night, bargain. 20 minutes to set up camp and a further 5 minutes to change and I was happily splashing up and down the pool as the only inhabitant, I don't think it is possible to beat a cooling swim after a few hours pedalling. A shower and an ice lolly completed my recuperation, and realising I was fairly hungry at this point decided to set out and find some lunch, and hopefully a place to enjoy an evening meal later. Never one to rely on modern technology I referred to my trusty map pages and found there was the small town of Junas only a kilometre or so up the road and off I set.

Possibly the strangest town I have ever visited, it appeared quite large but I could only find one bar and one shop, I say shop but it appeared to be closed and when it was open I got the impression it was more of a co-op where goods were exchanged rather than bought, weird, at least the bar seemed normal and sat outside opposite the church square a cold beer in hand talking to the waitress and two old gents was very convivial and informative, at least to the point of finding out that the bar was the only place worth eating out in town. After a second beer it seemed advisable to move on (or not move at all) and so following random signposts for the town of Congenies I had hoped of finding a bite of lunch. The first sign of life I came across was equally 'weird' in my view, just outside of what I perceived to be the town of Congenies was a partial building site upon which sat a large 'out of town' DIY / general household goods store, not so strange you might think but attached to it was a new Boulangerie/Pattiserie serving the widest variety of cakes/bread/sandwiches I had ever seen, with tables perched outside on effectively a building site. To me it was just so incongruous to find something so quintessentially French traditional in such an out of town location, maybe the plan was to move all the shops to this 'out of town' shopping park and the DIY and Boulangerie where the first to be built? Anyway it saved me riding into town and having to search, the delicacies on offer where worth travelling out of town for if you are ever in the area.

After a mid afternoon snooze and further dip in the pool I set off back to the bar in Junas for a spot of real fodder. I expected to eat outside on the covered pavement we had occupied earlier in the day so happily leant my trusty steed against the railings and wandered into the bar to see what delights were on offer. WOW what a culture shock, the outside of the place as I have mentioned was standard French run down village bar/cafe, stepping inside was like entering a dodgy 80's nightclub that was trying to attract stag/hen nights. The entire place was pitch black with deep purple decor from the seats to the drapes, even the pool table had purple baize. Even more incongruous for a town the size and location of Junas was a large dance floor in the far recess of the room complete with full array of disco lights and smoke machine. I was the only bugger there. The waitress from lunch time appeared behind the bar and I asked for a menu, she explained that the 'dining room' was upstairs and led me onto the roof of the building which housed approximately 30 tables laid out for dining and was partially covered by pergolas offering at least some shade if required. Wondering what sort of clientele frequented such a place I was more than a little concerned that I had left my only means of transport just leaning on the railings downstairs!! The menu consisted of pizza, burger, pizza and pizza. I opted for pizza. Why have the French with such a great culinary heritage opted to eat nothing but pizza when they dine out? To be fair the pizza was possibly one of the tastiest I have had, ever, and the first time I had ever eaten a pizza with a double cream base rather than tomato, surprisingly good.

Leaving the club, posters on the wall caught my eye and it appeared that bands played the club at regular intervals, I think I even recognised some of names, and my bike was still leaning against the railings, result! I decided to investigate further and enquiring back at the campsite turned up that Junas is the centre of the Jazz scene and hosts one of the biggest festivals going, with the bar I had visited also being a popular venue for touring groups. Who would have thought it? Once again the crickets all switched off cock on 10pm, except one who had to have the last word for nearly a minute longer.

Day 13

Managed something of a lie in and it wasn't until after 8am that I started to de-camp, the temperature was already a balmy 23° without a cloud in the sky. My breakfast rations had run out 5 days previously and I had simply never bothered to replace them on the basis that I expected to be always able to find a shop pretty much as soon as I set off. I thought I had hit the jackpot when I called into the office to pay for my nights stay, a fantastic array of croissant and pastries sat invitingly on the counter. After making my selection and in the act of taking the bagged up treats, it was then that they decided to check that they were what I had pre-ordered the night before, doh, the brekky treats disappeared faster than they had arrived. Never mind I was only about 5k from Sommieres and confident given the size of the place that a boulangerie would be easy to find.

My next overnight destination was a little over 100km away and I was due to stay in Bedarieux with Christian, found on the Couchsurfing web-site, but I would be a day early due to still having a day in lieu. Whilst in my contact with Christian I had arranged that I may be a day either side, the fact was that the next day was Bastille day, and as such I expected staying with a French family on this celebrated day could be quite an experience. It also helped that the Tour de France just happened to be crossing my route 50k down the road at around lunch time the next day, so it was an easy decision to cycle to where they intersected my route and then search for a campsite nearby, whoohoo another easy day, which given the expected temperature was more than welcome.

After a very easy ride back into Sommiere my faith in finding a patisserie was rewarded with the sight of a large window display of cakes and fancies as I rode through one of the many town squares, luckily I am a tight wad and checking my change discovered they had charged me twice what they should have, innocent mistake? Still the goodies persuaded me to give them the benefit of the doubt.

One of the strangest most abstract things I have ever come across presented itself a few miles out of town, cycling along at a steady pace I came upon a roundabout, checking to my left perfect tarmac stretched all of 20 meters into scrubland. No traffic coming either from across the roundabout or from this stretch of adjoining road I proceeded to cycle round, only to find the junction off to the right was also a 20 meter stretch of tarmac. This commuter route led straight toward a small copse of trees. Unable to believe my eyes there was also a pedestrian crossing over this short road, and anyone who took the junction (presumably because they had been on the vino) and had to turn round, would be presented with a full complement of road signs.

I was expecting an easy ride with relatively flat terrain unfortunately my route took me through the centre of the Cazevieille Pic Saint Loup, if I was to liken it to anything it would be a meteor strike, a large depression surrounded by a continuous donut of a hill. The road was barriered and as far as my school boy French could make out it was because the basin flooded. Not much chance of that in the 30º+ heat of the day but at least the surrounding wooded hillsides did something to offer shelter from the increasing wind.

Well before noon I rolled into Viols le Fort the closest town to my chosen spot for viewing the tour, it was closed, well at least the boulangerie and the only food shop where. As luck would have it sat nav said that the nearest Chambre de Hautes was closer to my viewing spot than the town so with only 35km and 450m of climbing in my legs I toddled off to kill two birds with one stone, recce my spot for the 'morrow and have a comfy room for the night.

The area I had chosen to view the tour from was a junction on the main road about 4km out of town, here the peloton would leave the 'main' drag and head off down a 'local' road, this should be the ideal spot, not only was it in the middle of nowhere with the nearest town being tiny, it would also mean the peloton should slow down to take the junction giving an ideal photo opportunity. Happy that I had found the place I had selected on google maps and happy that it would indeed be ideal, not least because it was on my route to Bedarieux, I headed off in the direction sat nav said to find my nights accommodation.

At least that was the theory, sat nav sent me down a narrow side road that turned into a track, thinking this must be wrong I turned round and went back to the juncion and tried again, no this was definitely where sat nav wanted me to go. Struggling along the track, resorting to pushing my laden bike to avoid punctures, sure enough a few hundred meters further through some trees I came upon a ramshackle farm house. OH well beggars can't be choosers, after much shouting and searching I found the owner in a run down hangar at the rear. Explaining in broken French that I wished to rent a room for the night and was this the Chambre de Hautes advertised from the road side and led to by my sat nav. Yes but yet again the place had closed its doors to paying customers years before, sorry they had never thought to remove the sign, probably because since the new owners had moved in, no one had actually tried to take a room before. I asked if it would be possible to camp in the garden and use the house for ablutions, but I fear I may have lost something in translation as I received a curt NON!

I have in the past considered buying property in France the prices in these rural areas are ridiculously cheap, considering the money I could sell my 3 bed terrace for, it would easily be possible to buy a 5 bed farmhouse complete with a couple of 'gites' thrown in for good measure, and have change. The dream would be to rent out rooms/gites whilst sitting in the sun next to a pool sipping Chateauneuf and doing bugger all apart from a bit of cycling. Reality as hit though considering that first the chambre in Vassieux-en-Vercors had closed its doors to paying guests and now this, maybe the market was saturated.

Back to the main road and to sat nav, after all it wasn't its fault that the place was shut, I had a two choices for campsites, back the way I had come for about 9 km to Saint Martine de Londres which appeared to be a sizable town , or off down the minor road the tour would be taking. Deciding by now I was a little peckish I opted to head for the former and stop in Viols in the hope somewhere had opened. No such luck only the bar was open, so I carried straight on. After passing through the town of St. Martine sat nav led me through a new housing estate and finished at a dead end, the road had been cut across by a new autoroute. Marvellous, no campsite, retracing my route to the centre of town and to a tourist information bureau I was belatedly informed that the campsite had been closed a number of years before to make way for the new road. Progress. No there was no replacement campsite. Well and truly fed up I could see myself wild camping at the roadside to watch the tour, never mind, back in Viols I had noted that the ubiquitous Pizza cafe would be open at t-time and there had been a been village green with public wc so I would be ok until I had to camp up. After riding round in circles now for over 30km I returned to Viols in early afternoon and straight to the bar. A liquid lunch! The temperature had been steadily climbing into the afternoon and whilst the beers seemed a little on the expensive side for a small town, the fact that each fresh drink came in a glass extracted from a deep freeze was most welcome.

After a couple or three I was beginning to feel decidedly drowzy, it was still only 2pm I had a while to wait for food and with nothing better to do I wheeled the bike off to the town green and sought shelter under a tree for a couple of hours snooze. It didn't seem like much later that I was awoken by the sound of children playing, whilst I had been asleep a couple of campervans had made home on the fars side of the green and the kids where running around, noisy bleeders. Anyway what is good for the goose, I decided if it was ok for them to park up then surely no one could object to me pitching my tent? To be on the safe side though I thought it best to enquire at the marie, out of politeness if nothing else. So back into the town square to the marie. The town square was a hive of activity with a stage being erected and trestle tables being set up everywhere, the marie was meant to be open according to the sign on the door, but the only person present was a surly cleaner who informed me they where shut. Sod it, I had tried, up with the tent and chain the bike up, hopefully it would still be there on my return from tea.

Returning once again to the town square, the stage was fully built and a van was now being unloaded of sack after sack of mussels. We were in the middle of the countryside, miles from the nearest coast , where do all these mussels come from? What is it with the French and mussels? Obviously it was a festival to celebrate Bastille day, albeit a day early. Finally sitting down for Pizza the waitress informed me there was to be a live band and mussels and frites later, I still decided to have a pizza though, which was at best mediocre. Sat outside the bar a hour or so later enjoying a nice cold drink I was soon surrounded by the local populace as they prepared to enjoy the festivities. It wasn't that I was made unwelcome, in fact I was told I was free to enjoy the food later that the commune was providing, but I was tired and very much out of my depth with the conversations that was taking place around me, so after a further drink I left for my tent.

Probably a mistake with hindsight I would have been better off staying and joining in, more so because the number of campervans had increased and what with screaming kids running round at 2am and the fireworks, sleep was a distant memory, at least I avoided a hangover, and felt my bike was safer from being next to it.

Day 14

No real need to rush this morning, I only had the few km to cycle to my view point and the tour wouldn't be going through until after lunch, plenty of time to get dressed, have a bite to eat and shop for lunch. The boulangerie that had been closed yesterday would be open this morning according to the sign so no worries. The first problem was the public loos, or lack of, sorry but I don't poo down a hole if I can help it! So once again I found myself looking for a cafe with a decent loo and soft bog paper, not that the latter was a problem, I was prepared with a packet of moist toilet tissue, the last thing I wanted on a 3 week bike ride was a stinging ring. The cafe come pizzaria did not open through the day, the bar was closed until 10am, they probably thought I was an alcoholic sat waiting at their outside tables when they arrived looking slightly worse for wear from last nights exertions. At least when they did finally open they served a decent cup of coffee and the condition of the convenience was an improvement on the public lavs. Next stop the boulangerie, and to stock up on drinks, sandwiches and sweet things to wait for the tour.

I soon arrived at my 'quiet' spot in the country. Only difference was now there where about 15 campervans squashed onto the triangle of grass that represented the junction and half a dozen Gendarmes marching around. I have to say that the French don't do things by halves, the campers had the full set up, with meals on the go and the tv's out on tables so they could follow the action. As the time went by more and more cars started to line the road after the junction and the crowd became several deep. This was quite a surprise given where we were and I decided it would be prudent to fasten the bike up a good way down the road in the direction of Bedarieux to allow me a quick getaway after the tour went by.

Once again the sun was out and the temperature was climbing, however today it was accompanied by a good strength wind, and from the chatter on the police radios it became evident that they where expecting the riders to be slightly delayed, this was a worry as I had 50km to ride to my evenings destination and this would be into the wind the entire distance, but I refused to miss the spectacle of the tour.

The next set back was the arrival of another cavalcade of Gendarmes with news that the caravan would not be coming through our little resting place, a decision had been made that the tour caravan would be taking the main roads in a direct route to the finish rather than risk getting stuck and blocking the route the riders had to take. So not only had my decision to watch the tour from a narrow 'side' road been confounded by unexpected crowds, I was now going to miss the spectacle (and freebies) of the caravan.

What was most surprising was the reaction of the many French supporters of the tour, as soon as word went round that the caravan would be bypassing our rural spot a good half of the campervans started packing up and moving off for the next point on the route where the caravan would pass. These same campervans where definitely not tour virgins, their cabins decked out with souvenir signs pinched from the road side of earlier stages. Wow, I thought, the freebies that are thrown out from the promotional vehicles must be pretty amazing to get this reaction, maybe the Skoda wagon chucked out keys to a new car? Anyway it meant the crowd had thinned out and seen as I had been there a couple of hours already there was no point in moving. Settling down on the verge for a picnic lunch it wasn't long after that the claxons could be heard from the first of many transits vans, with young mademoiselles adorned in yellow hanging off the back selling bags of tour goodies, and the annoying rattle of an overexcited monsieur extolling the virtues of une bag, une stilo, une carte etc etc for 20E god what a load of tat. Shortly after the first floats of the caravan arrived, laugh I nearly cried, all the work those people had put in to set up camp and then pack up again all for nothing, the race directors had decided the road was wide enough after all. Mind you what the excitement was all about is anyone's guess. Talk about tat, the thinnest cotton baseball caps, energy drink, mini cheeses and the odd keyring, that was what the freebies amounted to, and the spectators where literally fighting in lumps to scrabble after them. I got two caps a keyring and a lump of cheese. My best grab though was a blow up pillow advertising a French motel chain, should be useful despite the smell of cheap plastic.

From the departure of the last vehicle of the caravan it took nearly a further 2 hours for the cyclists to arrive, their approach signalled by the increasing number of police motorbikes and finally the thump of the tv helicopters. The breakaway was only a few seconds in front of the peloton and the ride past lasted seconds, travelling at such a speed that it was impossible to make out individual riders. Oh well the best laid plans, not waiting to watch the numerous support cars and hangers on I thought it was about time I set off on my own bike with over 50km to ride and the wind still building, if it had slowed the tour down what chance had I? It was already mid afternoon about a hour later than expected that I set off to Bedarieux.

The wind was even stronger than I had first thought and going was tediously slow, instead of taking a couple of hours I could see it taking three. My planned route took me on what looked like a scenic route around the Lac du Salagou, and despite the wind when the junction with the main road presented itself I saw no reason to disrupt my plan. Unfortunately the mapping gods and French farmers had other ideas, after a pleasant 20 minutes pedalling the road surface started to deteriorate, and deteriorate to the point I was off and pushing expecting the road to eventually improve, it didn't, it just ended in the middle of a field. Sat Nav had me located on a road, the physical map showed every turn and twist I had taken and showed me on a road. This was not recent and a problem of some outdated software or outdated map (both were new) no, sat in the middle of where the road should have run was a large mature tree! I give up, what took 30 minutes out took a further 30 minutes to return back to the main road so by now it was getting towards late afternoon with still a good distance to cycle into an increasingly strong wind. To compound matters the sat nav was constantly turning itself off as the internal battery had been allowed to run too low and I had run out of AA batteries and was having to resort to AAA in the usb charging unit that didn't seem to be cutting the mustard. Fortunately it was a straight run into Bedariux and I could remember from examining google street view prior to leaving that Christian lived just off the main road on my side of the town. Out of politeness I got on the phone to Christian and explained I would not arrive until early evening and was that ok or I could find a campsite if it put him out, he was brilliant and said he would be stood at the end of the street as it could be a little awkward to find his house.

On google street view my destination was a paint pealing gate in a broken down 10 foot wall, it didn't look particularly salubrious and I was unsure what to expect. As promised Christian was stood at the end of the street at the junction of the main road and flagged me down as I approached, he was not the young chap I had expected from his Couchsurfing profile but an elderly retired gent. Leading me through the garden gate we entered an oasis of gardens, and a large infinity style swimming pool surrounded by patio. The main house was a large renovated traditional stone affair but I was quickly shown to the guest/pool house that was to be my nights accommodation, complete with bedroom, bathroom, shower, kitchen and sitting room it was more than I could have reasonably expected. He told me he would give me chance to get showered and changed and then if I would like to join him and his wife on the patio for an aperitif they would be dining alfresco, I had been expecting Bastille day celebrations and mentioned to Christian that I hoped I was not disrupting any plans they may have had, but it would seem that many places celebrated the night before as I had witnessed in Viols.

For the first time I can honestly say conversation flowed freely, whether it was the fact I had been in France for a couple of weeks now so my vocabulary was increasing, or whether it was the fact both Christian and his wife spoke a little english (both being particularly well educated, she a retired teacher and him a retired executive of EDF) or whether it was in direct proportion to the amount of Pastis consumed?

The meal consisted of a remarkable stew (though it wasn't called stew) that I was led to believe was leftovers so had been no bother, and complemented by a marvellous glass or bottle or two of red. The cheese course, I was informed, had been made by their son, I am sure I saw the label and it was the same as some I had seen at the spa shop in Verdon, bloody marvellous Roqueforte either way. Just before turning in for the night I was presented with a fourfoot sock containing a fresh baguette for morning and told to help myself to anything I could find in the kitchen fridge. Retiring to the pool house I decided it would be a good idea to rinse out my dirty washing in the sink and leave it to dry overnight whilst I had the opportunity. Sleep was very quick coming.

Day 15

Woke up fresh and early, which was quite a surprise given the amount of pastis and wine that had been consumed the previous evening, the weather had turned from glorious cloudless blue skies to a greyish overcast hue with sporadic light rain. Despite this I was hell bent on making full use of the available facilities so the first thing was to dive into the pool and enjoy a good swim along with the 'stingray' pool cleaner scouring the bottom. Next business was to enjoy a warm leisurely shower, this was marred somewhat by the shower hose coming away from the shower head, I didn't do it, honestly Christian.

The fridge was stacked with all sorts of compots, spreads, yoghurts and cheeses, so taking my host to his word I tucked into a breakfast fit for a king that would mean I had no need to find food until evening. My previous nights washing was not quite dry but the rain had abated so hopefully packing it in mesh washing bags and hanging them off the back of the pannier would finish them off. I was just wondering on what etiquette to use as I was eager to get off but there was no sign of my host, when he suddenly appeared in his dressing gown, I think he was a little taken aback by my early departure especially on a Sunday morning. I am not sure if the baguette was all for me or if he was expecting to join me for breakfast either, ah well it was very nice.

The clouds where soon dispersed by the wind and despite the wind the temperature was soon heading into the thirties, at least my washing would soon dry! The sat nav continued to play up and I resorted to turning it on, checking the route to see if I needed to turn off anytime soon and then going on. It wasn't until I reached Saint Pons de Thomieres that I found an open Tabac that sold AA batteries, got to love France on a Sunday!

I was expecting an easy day with flat terrain having left the Alps far behind and the Pyrenees not yet visible on the horizon, the wind was meant to be my only foe. I think the rest of the area is flat, North East of Carcassonne, but not my route, oh no I had hills. The Col de

Serrieres at 678m and the Col de Salettes at 886m and they seemed to be the stomping ground of local cyclists looking for a challenge. Now after the Bonnette at 2802m and even Ventoux at 1912m these two might sound like a walk in the park but when you consider Holme Moss is only 524m and even Snowden is only 1085m then these two Cols are put into perspective.

Despite stuffing my face at brekky by noon the wind and the second Col were beginning to take their toll on my energy levels. A friendly 'roadie' came steaming up and as is a cyclists way he slowed and enquired to how I was going on and where I was going and where I had been loaded up to the gills. I told him and he said I was in luck as the next village just over the brow held a market every Sunday and sold a multitude of delights to tempt the hungry cyclist, with a wave he was off.

Now I think he must have been taking a different route off that mountain because I never came across a village, market or not. What I did find was a street, in the middle of nowhere, with a community hall/shop. The stonework over the door gave the legend 'Lespinassiere Secular School for Boys' and seeing life beyond the windows I decided it was as good a place to stop as any. Inside the hall there where dozens of tables set out for dining with a few ladies bustling around setting out plates and others could be seen slaving over bubbling cauldrons. Unsure that I would be welcome I made my way to the attached 'shop' a room with wooden shelves laden with all manner of food stuffs and household items, it was shut! Well no one was serving in there, the food hall, I think a 1960's holiday camp had a counter at the far end complete with silver tea urn, think of the cafe from 'Last of the Summer Wine' and you won't be far off. Anyway one of the ladies shuffled out to serve me a glass of milk and a couple of bars of chocolate. By now the hall was beginning to fill with families of all ages in their Sunday best. I didn't like to ask if there was room for one more and I was getting strange looks as it was dressed in lycra. Maybe it was a regular Sunday lunch or maybe it was an extension of the Bastille Day celebrations, either way I thanked the ladies and made my escape.

Over the final stretch into Caunes Minervois, my days destination, the temperature had risen to the mid thirties and the wind continued to gain in ferocity, this compounded by the landscape that was becoming decidedly dustier. The campsite just out of town looked quite inviting with what appeared to be large clean shower blocks, a small take-away 'hut' and office building, no pool, but individual pitches surrounded by four foot hedging as a windbreak.

I was informed to pick any pitch and left to my own devices after paying over a few euro. The ground was rock hard and crumbled as soon as a peg was attempted to be driven in, finally I resorting to tying up to collected rocks and the hedge I hoped the tent wouldn't blow away. Next job with all the wind and dust my poor stead needed a bit of attention, the chain cleaning and oiling, the front and rear tyres swapping over and given a few extra psi, other than that the brakes were still in good condition and everything was running smooth, the fact that every night I had been giving her the once over with GT85 before the ravishes of a night outside must have been doing a good job.

A very sweaty lay down with a short snooze and a read revitalized me enough for an evening of wandering around the town in search of some local delicacy, please no more Pizza! I think the one item of extras I would recommend to anyone is a kindle. The battery was good for a couple of hours reading a day, it weighs much less than a book, and my old wireless model gives me free internet access on amazons network for checking such things as the weather.

A warm shower to wash off the dust and sweat and into the glad rags I was ready to hit the town. I like to wander around new places and check out everything and everywhere and what they have to offer, both menus and prices, sometimes I still pick the wrong restaurant though, expecting to get what is described on the menu being my main downfall! Caunes appears to be quite a large town, especially compared to most of the others I have passed through and wandering round took an enjoyable couple of hours including a couple of beers sat in the market square. I had opted to return to a rather large fine looking house for my evening meal with a menu that promised local cuisine at prices that where neither cheap nor eye watering. The meal was poor, maybe it was my fault, I chose to try Cassoulet for the first time expecting a rich meaty stew, instead I got a foul smelling watery slop that was all pork skin and beans, feeling very let down I returned to the camp and with relief saw the takeaway hut was open and bought a large portion of chips to enjoy in the comfort of my tent. Not the most entertaining or interesting of days, perversely whilst I hadn't enjoyed the two climbs today I was missing the Alps.

Day 16

After using all my made back days I had two choices today, cycle the 90km to Varhiles and stop with a commune I had found on Couchsurfing, or continue on and do 120 km and stop to the West of La Bastide de Serou. The former would give me a short following day and allow some sightseeing at a nearby grotto or make a day ready for meeting the tour again at the top of the Peyseroude.

Having seen the shambles of the tour a few days previous and knowing that it had to pass over the Peyseroude on two consecutive days I decided to make a day and rang the kind lady in Varhiles to tell her I would no longer be visiting, from the sounds of children screaming and crying in the background it was the correct decision!

The morning started off hot and windy with the temperature already heading toward 20° as I set off. During my morning ablutions I had exhausted both my sun tan cream and toothpaste so the first port of call was going to be a pharmacist a Caunes. Never go to a pharmacist in France for these items, toothpaste was marked up at 7.9Euro and suntan lotion nearly 20 Euro for a small tube. I declined the proffered articles and made my escape hoping to find somewhere cheaper on route.

Today, according to the profile on sat nav, was going to be much flatter, circling around the North of Carcassonne and off to the West towards the Pyrenees. Naturally the wind was not dropping so the fact that the terrain was less challenging was offset by the gusting head wind. The scenery in the early half of the route was more industrial and bland than anything else passing rugby fields was the highlight.

Shortly before noon I came across a shop in the middle of nowhere, a sort of out of town convenience store but no larger than an average petrol station. I managed to pick up some cheap toothpaste, suntan cream, a baguette and a bar of chocolate.

Lunch was had at the side of the road and consisted of a dry baguette and a bar of melted chocolate in a gale force wind, today could only get better!

So it did, crossing over into the Department de l'Ariege, the wind dropped and the scenery improved to cycling through countless fields of sunflowers, the temperature had risen to 33° and on the horizon I got my first view of the Pyrenees, something to aim towards and look forward to. The Pas du Portel at 498m was my only challenge this afternoon and was a pleasant change to flat riding against the wind.

By mid afternoon I had passed through Varhiles and approaching Bastide, the closest town to where Cecile lived, my hostess for the night. I noted a large attractive looking campsite with a pool and very nearly stopped rather than continuing on to her house. I had problems finding her house on google maps during my planning, it was located down a track off the main road in the middle of nowhere, the track didn't seem to exist but from google earth it would appear to run down the side of a graveyard!
After cycling over 100km in the wind and heat a cafe was a welcome sight so I decided to stop and enjoy a leisurely beer or two before searching for her house. They must have been expecting a good trade later on judging by the buckets of potatoes that the woman was peeling sat outside at one of the tables, it seemed unfair to disturb her for a second time when I wanted a refill.

Checking the sat nav and map I judged that the turn off for Ceciles was 20km down the road, so setting the computer to count down this distance so I would know when I would be about there, I set off.

Ceciles house proved hard to find, in fact I cycled a good 5km past the turn off and arrived at another junction on the opposite side of the road before I realised I had gone too far, I think I must have set the sat nav in miles instead of KM, oops. Still every cloud. Taking the junction in order to turn round I spotted what looked like a low slung large hut, strung with fairy lights, being inquisitive as to what the hell this could be in the middle of nowhere I parked the bike up and had a wander round. It turned out to be a restaurant, it was a wood hut, most of the tables where inside but there was no roof and the menu consisted of nothing but duck. It promised to open in a couple of hours so not of much use to me.

Cycling back along the main road I eventually spotted a run down church set back from the road with a narrow track running up the side, this must be the way to Ceciles, surely? The track did indeed lead to a row of buildings, but there was no sign of life. Thinking it best to ring Cecile rather than starting to bang on doors, and if there was no answer to ride back to the campsite before it got too late. Cecile answered the phone pretty much straight away and luckily her English was better than my French!

Originally when organising my stopover I had said I could arrive either tonight or the following night, so I wasn't feeling bad about cancelling my night in Vahiles, unfortunately it turned out that Cecile had rather been hoping I would turn up the next night, she had been called away by work to Toulouse and wouldn't be returning to home until the last train which meant after midnight. I told her not to worry and I would head off for the campsite down the road. Amazingly she said not to be so silly and that as I was looking at the building her house was the second along with the blue door, it was open and I should make myself at home, help myself to any food and that the spare bedroom was on the second floor with the mattress stood in the corner, she would see me for breakfast! So here was a single young lady living in the middle of nowhere who didn't lock her door and was trusting enough to have a strange bloke turn up and sleep in her house when she hadn't met them and wasn't even due to return until the middle of the night!! Not sure if I was the scared one!

The kitchen was rural to put it politely, with no obvious signs of food other than veg and a bag of crisps, so after making my bed and taking a nice hot bath I was back on my bike and heading off to see if the duck restaurant had actually opened for the evening. Unsurprisingly I was the only diner, but it was well worth the trip, I went the whole hog and had the signature dish of duck. It consisted of foie gras, duck sausage, duck breast, duck pate, duck leg, in fact just about every variation of duck you could imagine, lovely. Luckily I had taken lights with me for tunnels because by the time I arrived back at Cecile's it was dark.

Day 17

I had a good nights sleep on a proper mattress and had not been disturbed by Cecile returning home, in fact once again I was unsure about etiquette. I had never met my host so I could hardly get up and disappear without speaking, on the other hand I didn't want to be stuck here all day, and then was the worry of what to do if Cecile hadn't returned! Fortunately she was an early riser and I sound heard noises coming from the adjoining bedroom, waiting until I had heard her descend the stairs I got up made the bed and packed ready for off, Cecile was waiting at the dining table, breakfast consisted of herbal tea. Making my excuses that I had a long journey I thanked her for her hospitality and headed out, her final act was to present me with a bag of radishes to keep my energy up on the journey. Thanks Cecile.

The morning started a little cooler than I had become used to at only 7º and there was no wind, I was looking forward to a pleasant days cycling with a couple of climbs thrown in, tonight I had the choice of camping in Saint Beat or continuing on to Marignac and stopping with another Couchsurfing host Phillipe. Originally the plan had been to camp tonight, watch the tour, then go on to Phillipes before crossing the Peyserourde, but with the tour crossing the Col on both days I was thinking the option of going straight to Phillipes would be a better idea and getting over the Col on the first day, providing he could host me a day early.

The ride to the first Col of the day was pleasant and uneventful, passing into the Haute-Garonne the sunflower fields gave way wooded slopes and as the road became more sheltered the temperature increased. The Col de Portet d'Aspet at 1069m was a good muscle warmer after the last couple of days and the descent towards the Col de Mente with a slope of 17% certainly warmed the rims of the bike as the brakes tried to keep the speed down.

The Col de Mente traversed from the East is very well sheltered meaning there was not a breath of wind, whilst only 1349 m at its peak the road is a series of steep switchbacks and with the temperature climbing into the 40's this was going to be one of the biggest challenges of the trip. To be quite frank by the halfway point I was struggling, and opted to have a bit of a push to use some alternative muscle groups. As it happened there was an organised tour on the Mente, a large group of cyclists being supported by a mini-bus, and as I was pushing the bus stopped and offered to relieve me of my panniers and transport them to their meeting point on the summit, whilst the idea appealed it seemed even more of a cheat than pushing for a few meters so I declined.

One of the participants of the tour must have also got into difficulty and called up the minibus because a couple of corners further on I saw the bus pull up and execute a 3 point turn to head off back down the Col, unfortunately they misjudged the width of the road and managed to put the rear wheels off the tarmac and ground the underneath of the bus on the road surface, luckily they weren't overhanging a cliff face like the Italian Job but it wasn't a predicament I would want to be in. There was already a group of three or four vehicles stopped helping to try and see-saw the vehicle to get the front wheels on the ground to give traction but their attempts seemed pretty futile. At my next rest stop a couple of hairpins from the top the minibus finally passed me again so evidently they had managed and all had ended well.

France must be a popular destination for Australian cyclists because it was another pair of Aussie tourers that stopped to chat on their way across France to Cannes, I thought I had been carrying enough gear on my trip but one of them had managed to pack a full size DSLR and a couple of lenses, I wouldn't fancy carting my camera kit round and was quite happy with the tiny Nikon automatic!

At last the summit arrived and I could look forward to several miles of cooling breeze and not having to turn a pedal all the way into Saint Beat. Whilst the roads were quiet the campsite looked packed, obviously in preparation for the Tour passing close by on the following days, and cemented my resolve to call Phillipe and arrange a bed a night early. Next thing on the agenda was to find a cafe and get something cold, the isotonic fluid in the bladder in my backpack was now approaching the temperature of warm tea, having been exposed to the midday sun and heat coming from my back! Gratefully slumping into a relatively comfy iron chair in (on?) a pavement cafe I deferred from my first choice of beer and opted for a speciality limited edition magnum ice cream (in fact at only 1.5 Euro I had two, black cherry if you are interested, bargain) deciding that in the heat and with a few kilometres still to ride into Marignac I didn't want to suffer the headache that had threatened the day previous after my late afternoon session. Whilst sat out I was joined at an adjoining table by a couple of cyclists on their cafe stop, and luckily they spoke a smattering of English. One of the great advantages of travelling round on a fully loaded touring road bike is that it is a fantastic ice breaker, other tourers will always acknowledge you or stop for a chinwag, and so will most roadies, wanting to know how heavy the bike is, or if you are stopped is there a problem and can they help, cyclists are a great bunch.

Anyway I digress, after the usual expression of shock after they had tested the weight of my machine they were even more amazed to learn of my route. They were in town to see the tour with one of them living close by, but his friend had travelled over from a small town in the Langudoc and his ambition was to tackle Ventoux that was pretty much on his doorstep. I hope I gave him the required inspiration and confidence to get on with it!

Phillipe had said he was only too happy for me to arrive a day early and promised to ride out and meet me on the road from Saint Beat as whilst his town was small he lived tucked out of the way down an alley. Sure enough good to his word Phillipe was practically in Saint Beat by the time I had set off and left my companions to finish their rest stop.

Marignac was a small town as promised and was obviously in a state of quiet excitement about the Tour passing through, Phillipes house was off the main road (the only road for that matter) and was accessed firstly through a carport and finally a garage. Phillipe and his family were obviously sporting fanatics as in order to get through to the house door it was a fight past an assortment of bikes, kayaks, snowboards and skis. The house itself was on several levels and I was told I would be sleeping on the mezzanine (that looked more like an attic trap door) accessed by a rope ladder. After a brief introduction to his wife and children we plonked down in the kitchen and over a couple of beers he explained that it was good that I had rang when I did as the family where in the process of packing as they where leaving on a three month sabbatical in a couple of days. Through Couchsurfing they had a series of hosts arranged and where heading off to the Himalayas to help with an aid project and to do a bit of climbing!!

Evening meal was to be a home made curry, the first curry (and last) I have come across in my travels round France, and it smelled fantastic as he prepared it. The meal was to be taken outside in the garden and it was as we were sitting down, with my mouth salivating in anticipation, that Phillipe received a phone call. With apologies he asked if we would all mind postponing the meal as he was going to have to drive the few miles to the train station to pick up Matt. Matt was an Australian (yes another of the buggers) that was touring Europe for the year and had arranged (through Couchsurfing) to stay the night, he was also a night early. (I had to admire this family, in all the confusion and hassle of packing and organising a family 'vacation' they still had the time to host strangers who couldn't even keep to a schedule!!)

It was a truly memorable evening, not only was the food and drink top notch so was the conversation. I thought I had been pretty adventurous over the last couple of weeks cycling around 900 miles across the Alps but it was a struggle to match the exploits of Matt on his previous 7 months of touring Europe, or Phillipe with his vast experience of mountaineering, caving, and skiing!

Like all good things the evening soon came to an end, well it did for me, I was falling asleep after the exertion of the Col de Mente, whilst Matt was still alive and kicking having only suffered a train journey from Paris. My mezzanine 'bedroom' was directly above the living room so I happily volunteered to kip in the downstairs hall on a sofa bed and left them to it (and Matt to the rope ladder!!)

Day 18

Breakfast was traditional coffee and croissants with ham and cheeses thrown in for good measure. Matt added to the repast with a jar of Vegamite that he was carrying round to remind him of home? Very much like marmite but not as nice, prefer meat extract to Veg! Matt was staying with Phillipe that night and listening to my plans the previous evening had taken up the offer to borrow an old bike and join me up the Peyserourde to watch the tour. He wasn't new to cycling but I thought it pretty brave to tackle the pass on a strange bike without any recent conditioning. Phillipe meanwhile was also going cycling with friends as it would be his last opportunity for a few months, not interested in the crowds associated with the tour though he was heading out in the opposite direction on local roads that he knew.   Firstly though he cycled with us to the local supermarket so we might stock up on a few provisions for the day.

Butter, a baguette, tomatoes and a slab of chocolate, the joy of having panniers, poor Matt had to make do with a bag of gums.

Whilst I was travelling loaded up to the gills Matt was on a lightweight Bianci and he had no problem following me into Bagneres-de-luchon, the town at the foot of the Col de Peyserourde and today's finish line for the tour. What a sight, hundreds of HGV and coaches and barriers everywhere, there was enough firepower on display with the Gendarmes to settle a small war. Fortunately whilst the roads had already been closed to motorised traffic, noone had any objections to cyclists and pedestrians. It was like a parade with the number of people making their way up toward the summit on foot and two wheels. Now that Matt knew where he was going it was my turn to try and keep up and it wasn't long before he took off on the wheel of a gang of roadies. Happy to maintain my own pace I settled into a steady rhythm, overtaking some, being left for dead by others. On the higher slopes the road started to become lined with countless number of campervans and even a tented village had sprung up with a marquee offering food and drink for those stopping overnight. As the number of pedestrians increased and the road narrowed from the campers parked either side the going was getting more and more perilous having to wind in and around groups of pedestrians carrying everything from cool boxes to deckchairs.

Compensation for the crowds, the temperature, and the incline came from the electric atmosphere, the fact I was slogging up this mountain on a fully loaded bike obviously resonated with many of them as cry's of 'bonne courage' and 'allez allez' started to ring in my ears giving more energy than any gel ever could. Passing one group of staggering revellers carrying a large cool box between them I heard them say in English "bloody hell wouldn't fancy riding that up this" with a sly smile I shot back over my shoulder "no me neither"

Fortunately one side effect of cycling up was that I arrived at the summit well before most pedestrians and was able to pick my own spot, just after the summit line marker on the descent side. By now the sun was at its zenith and the tarmac was beginning to feel decidedly sticky, there was no sign of Matt so I bedded in to eat my lunch and wait for the caravan. The sun had grown so hot my cheese had become spreadable, but it was jolly tasty. I must have been sat a good hour before Matt turned up, no idea where I passed him but he had blown up on the lower slopes and stopped for a rest.

With still no sight of the caravan but with the crowds increasing it just meant taking turns to visit the summit cafe for cold drinks whilst the other kept our place and watched the gear. We had made good time to the summit, which whilst affording a good spot meant it was a good four hours before the helicopters could be heard across the valley and the first vehicles of the caravan came into sight. Once again it was carnage as the freebies started hitting the tarmac and the scrabbling began.

God knows where everyone had been hiding but by the time the leaders appeared over the summit the crowds had swollen 4 deep. Unlike on the climbing side where the spectators are virtually left to do their own thing, on the descent side the Gendarmes where keen to make sure the accelerating peloton had room to move, with armed officers spaced every few yards holding back the throng I wasn't about to argue. Maybe I am just too British as many of the continental fans had no problems pushing back and continually ignoring their orders, stepping in front of the gun toting coppers for a better view. Probably because we are not used to every policemen carrying a 45mm cannon or an AK47, mind you it didn't stop the officer in front of me from whipping out his instamatic and snapping off a few piccies himself, so all in all it was a very amiable situation and my respect went to the French authorities for the way the event was controlled without strong arm tactics.

As soon as the last of the team cars had passed by I bid farewell to Matt and headed off in the direction from which the tour had come, expecting crowds departing the mountain was expecting quite a melee. I was not disappointed, the first obstacle was the police. I had not expected the number of cyclists that wished to follow the route of the tour and upwards of 200 cyclists where being held by rapidly moved barriers across the road at the summit point, naturally I was cycling against this tide. After sitting around for a few minutes I approached a Gendarme and explained I was trying to cycle in the opposite direction, much to the consternation of the crowd he allowed me through the barrier and proceeded to part the massed ranks of roadies.

Many of the campervans where staying on the mountain side in preparation for the tour passing the following day, so that was one obstacle I didn't have to avoid, also on the West side there where fewer pedestrians, just cars and bikes to dodge then. In fact it was just a traffic jam! Time was passing and I had a fair few kilometres to travel and yet again I was going to have to contact my host, Julie, to see if she could put me up a night early, so realising that there should be no traffic coming up the mountain I pulled onto the wrong side of the road and let fly. All was going well and I was probably allowing my speed to creep a little high, overtaking countless vehicles of sweating and swearing individuals. Unfortunately a motorcyclist must have had the same idea and without checking his mirror suddenly pulled out into my path on a fast sweeping corner. I don't know who was shocked the most, me by a motorbike suddenly veering into my path, or him by a pushbike, with a shouting fat bloke onboard, overtaking between himself and the line of traffic at what must have been approaching 50 miles an hour. Despite being shook up myself and slowing my mad descent, it must have given him more food for thought as he never caught up. For the last few days my lucky mascot of a stuffed greyhound had been travelling fixed to the top of my bar bag, it wasn't until I stopped several kilometres after the terrain flattened to phone Julie that I realised he had been ejected and become the casualty of my rapid descent.

Julie lived in the small town of Bazus-Aure, a twenty minute detour off my route, but the closest 'Couchsurfer' I had been able to find. In our communication I gathered she was a young recently married lady and he husband was an excellent cook who was looking forward to feeding me. Or so the plan went, ringing a day early she was slightly hesitant as she explained her husband was away working and wouldn't be returning until the following afternoon. I apologised and said it would be no problem and that I understood and would be quite happy if she could recommend a campsite or allow me to pitch up in her garden. Obviously her mind made up she decided it wasn't a problem and to ring again when I was outside so she could open the electric gates.

The house and grounds where extensive and recently mostly renovated, her hubby it turned out was a builder and the property had been given to them by her parents, for renovation, which he was doing. She showed me into a light comfy bedroom and said to join her for tea when I was ready, saying it wouldn't be much as I wasn't expected. If the 3 course meal and drinks she provided are what unexpected guests receive I can only imagine what I would have been served had I arrived on time. Over the meal she offered to do my washing, and even though I only had a few days left to cycle it was an offer I couldn't refuse, especially as I fully expected everything to be dry by the following morning. She also asked if I would like to go to a concert, a band she liked was playing, she told me, in a village about 20 miles away, not wanting to put her out and being rather tired I declined, only with hindsight did I think that maybe I was a little rude and hadn't thought that it could be she wanted to go but wanted someone to travel with.

Unfortunately the evening was a little awkward, I was the first stranger she had ever hosted from the website and I think she was less than comfortable having a strange man in her house without her husband, the language barrier didn't help and I made my excuses to go to bed as soon as politeness allowed.

Day 19

This morning Julie was up and about and by the time I had showered and got myself downstairs she had breakfast laid out and waiting, all I had to do was let her know how I liked my coffee. Overnight the weather had changed and outside was a dull grey with low cloud and the real threat of torrential rain. She apologised and said unfortunately my washing that she had hung out in the open hangar the night before had failed to dry but it shouldn't be long as she had popped it in the dryer. I think she was slightly relieved to not have been murdered in her bed and she was much more relaxed and talkative, offering me a bed for a further night if I didn't want to venture out into the rapidly descending cloud that was now precipitating around us, the temperature was struggling to reach double figures.

Though I very much appreciated the offer of a bed for a further night, I was unwilling to squander my made day in case the weather deteriorated further and made the crossing of the Aspin and the Tourmalet in the same day compulsory, and there where a couple of further circular rides I fancied trying if it did improve. So complete with leg and arm warmers, gilet and full waterproofs I headed off into the cloud and drizzle.

The first challenge was the Col d'Aspin, a climb I had been looking forward to, only 12km long it rises 800m to an altitude of 1490m so whilst relatively short, compared to the Alps, at an average 7% gradient it is not to be underestimated. I am sure that the Aspin on a clear day must be one of the most beautiful routes around to cycle, however today I never managed break out of the low clouds and had to make do with the flora and fauna at the roadside and the numerous mini waterfalls. Despite the cloud, wrapped in many layers and waterproof jacket, the exertion of the climb meant I was overheating well before the summit, and probably just as wet as I would have been without, particularly as the drizzle had stopped, at least I had taken off the over trousers.

The sat nav was fully charged ready for the days ride, this was a plus as I was down to my last set of AA batteries, and in a moment of extreme optimism I had set the solar panel on the back of the panniers and wired it to hopefully trickle charge and keep the sat nav topped up. At the summit, and still in thick cloud, I was met by half a dozen camper vans left over from the tours passing from the previous day, and a group of four cyclists all in shorts and short sleeves. Hearing them speak English I asked if it would be possible for them to take my picture, you guessed it, they where all Aussies!

Expressing amazement that I had met even more of our antipodean cousins, and asking if Aussies were in fact in the process of invading France, elicited the response that they were amazed to find a solitary pom, dressed for snow, carrying everything bar the kitchen sink, with a solar panel stuck to the back of the bike in thick fog. Hmm maybe they had a point.

The descent was treacherous, not only was the road damp, my brakes ineffective, I was also frozen to the core from the wind chill on my previously overheated body. Seeing the welcome sight of chairs and umbrellas at the side of the road I stopped at the Auberge la Bergerie and ordered a large coffee to try and warm up. There where a few elderly locals in the cafe and I think the site of me caused a bit of head scratching, and when one of them wandered out and picked the bike up testing its weight the look on his face spoke a thousand words, which was good, because the speed and dialect they were talking had lost me at Bonjour!

I had meant to camp tonight in the valley between the Aspin and the Tourmalet, and had selected a campsite on google street view that appeared well appointed complete with pool and water slide, sure enough I was soon riding past the location and it was exactly as advertised. Without even contemplating stopping I continued riding past, there was no way I was going to start setting up camp in this weather and have to sit around for an afternoon in the middle of nowhere in a damp tent, with wet clothes, the pool would certainly have been out of the question. No I decided to continue into Sainte Marie de Campan, now on the Tacx I have a video ride of the Tourmalet and the start of the ride is in the town of SM de Campan, so I was fairly confident that I had seen a hotel.

Riding through the town the first structure I recognised was (I think) an old wash house, open on three sides with a solid roof it looked like as good a place as any to fasten the bike up and have a dry down and change of jersey. The cloud wasn't quite as dense in the town as it had been on the Aspin and the ambient temperature seemed to have risen slightly, though that could just be my body warming up from the icy descent. The structure I had thought was a hotel wasn't and I couldn't find so much as a shop open, it was like a ghost town, I knew there was another campsite a few km on toward the Tourmalet but I was beginning to think I would be better just riding on and getting over the last 'compulsory' climb of my trip. Again thinking that as I was already damp and not knowing if the weather would deteriorate further the next day it seemed like a good idea, adding the Tourmalet onto the Aspin would only give a climb for the day the same length of many of the Alpine climbs I had already tackled on the trip, and much shorter than many of the complete days I had in the Alps so should be a relatively simple challenge?

The cloud was not clearing as I started my ascent of the Tourmalet and I was resigned to having my view once again restricted to the roadside. As the energy began to drain from my legs I started to take more notice of the road signs, summit in 10km, altitude 1215, summit 2115m gradient 8.5%. Or in other words between here and the top the gradient was going to be 9% average, given I was on 8.5% at the moment the next 10 km could only get harder! I felt quite good passing a poor chap getting his breath on a roadside wall, his mountain bike leaning next to him already on the largest sprocket and smallest chain ring, at least I wasn't having to resort beyond 36 X 34 (more because after the farce on the Izoard I new dropping to the 24 tooth chain ring meant never setting off again than anything else) but at least it made me feel better.

Of course it wasn't long before the temptation of stopping to take a photo got too much, even in dense cloud the excuse to take a quick rest works for me! And of course the mountain biker then got his own back, this continued for the next few km with us leapfrogging one another as the other took a rest until we arrived at the place just before La Mongie where the road enters a protective gallery, at this point the cloud started to thin out and we both stopped at the same time to appreciate the feel of sun for the first time today. It turned out the guy was British and with friends who had left him some while ago, he had been climbing the Tourmalet all morning and was shocked to find out where I had started my day.

With the promise of clear blue skies I removed my jacket, leg and arm warmers and continued the climb, passing through La Mongie, the biggest concrete eyesore since Vars, I finally broke through the cloud completely to be left in bright sunshine in a cloudless blue sky, the temperature was soon climbing into the low 30's. With renewed vigour and energy it was the last I saw of my mountain biking compatriot. From just below La Mongie the average gradient increases to a leg killing 10% with long sections of 11% thrown in for good measure, these Pyrenean climbs might be shorter than their Alpine cousins but I think the gradients are worse and for this reason I am declaring the Tourmalet the hardest climb of my trip.

The final leg to the summit still had quite a few people sunning themselves outside parked campervans at the roadside (the tour had traversed the previous day) and once again my adrenalin levels were boosted by the calls of encouragement. The effort was well worth it, especially in the poor weather, the view from the summit was spectacular with the cloud lying over the entire valley on both sides with just the peaks of the surrounding mountains being visible. I had not realised what good time I had made and it was still only just after noon so it seemed criminal not to treat myself to a slap up lunch in the restaurant at the summit.

Looking down the valley toward where Luz-Saint-Saviour lay buried in cloud I was soon donning my arm and leg warmers again along with the lightweight jacket, I doubted much energy was going to be required on the descent and the wind chill would be paralysing otherwise. The ribbon of tarmac spread out before me, the scene of the tours ascent the day previous, would not only be damp once I entered the cloud layer, it was also covered in the multi coloured lettering and drawings of the spectators, including a shoal? of sperm swimming their way around one hairpin bend, I had heard talk in the restaurant that this could be particularly slippery.

Possibly the strangest sight met me around the first corner on the descent (shoal of sperm excepted) a Czech coach was parked in a layby and was offloading a group of cyclists and their bikes, well I suppose its easier than cycling up, and the descent is probably more fun, but it does rather defeat the point!!

The descent was not as perilous as I had led myself to believe and I impressed myself with the speed I managed to sustain once the first acute hairpins had been dispensed with. In fact I was going so fast I sailed straight past the turning I would have needed to take to head in to Viella in order to stay with my next host, I couldn't even use the low cloud as an excuse as I was now at the lowest point of the day and had passed through and under the clouds. Dropping into Luz and checking the sat nav I found that I had the option of cycling back up the Tourmalet a few km and contacting Anne to see if I might stay a night early or finding a campsite in Luz, again the sat nav said there was a site a few hundred meters along the main road. I knew from my contact with Anne via email that even stopping the following night was not set in stone as she had said she had many commitments around the date so I decided it would be best to just continue to the campsite and as it was now quite warm despite being dull and overcast it wouldn't be too much of a hardship. Luckily the campsite had a pitch vacant and after setting up camp, having a shower and getting changed into clean dry clothes I set off for a walk into the town centre to find somewhere to dine in the evening.

It was now about 3pm and the clouds were finally being dispersed by the sun and the walk in to town was a pleasant stroll in shirtsleeves. Luz is a small town with a pleasant town square surrounded by cafes, coffee shops, and delicatessens, and after a relaxing hour or so and a couple of beers I set off to see what the various eateries had to offer. On the town square there were three to choose from, two pizzerias and another who's main offering apart from sandwiches was .... pizza. Obviously a search further afield was in order. The hotels that I saw were offering nothing that appealed, the one other restaurant I found that I really liked the sound of despite the price on further examination required me to be eating as a couple. Everything on the menu that I fancied was for two to share, don't restaurateurs understand that a single diner might be partial to a nice fondue!! Of course I managed to locate a further two, yes you read it right at least 5 pizza serving emporiums in the one small French town, at least one looked a cut above the rest and vaguely more French than the others, with the entrees and puddings sounding at least like they were derived in this country. The only problem was it didn't open until 7pm so a good couple of hours to kill, the options were to trek back to the campsite and have a snooze, or back to the town square and people watch in the sun over a few more beers, the latter won out on the basis that tomorrow I didn't have to be anywhere if I didn't want to be.

It is a good job I was waiting on the doorstep at seven o clock ready for a meal as I was informed they were virtually booked out for the evening. After three weeks my French had improved to the point where it was as good as it had ever been and I was pleased to not only be able to read the menu, understand it, but also make a reasonable hash of ordering my first two courses with beers and wine in what must have been passable French to the waiter, though as it turned out I need not have worried. The reason the restaurant was booked out was a family of Ex-pat English and French were celebrating their young daughters birthday. Having nothing better to do but earwig the conversation I gathered that the owner was friends of the ex-pats being originally from, I think, Huddersfield himself and married to a French lady. This was only evident when he was talking to the elderly English grandparents as the rest of the time he was speaking fluent French with the same regional accent I had heard the locals talking with.

I was just about finished with my entree, and conversing with the waiter in French when another English family came into the restaurant and where shown to the adjacent table, mum, dad, teenage son and daughter. It was bloody embarrassing, they weren't dressed like yobs, and on first impressions you would have to guess they were middle class, going on about coming back for the skiing in the winter yadda yadda yadda, however they didn't speak a word of French and obviously believed that there was no possibility that anyone would understand English unless it was spoken exceptionally slowly and loudly. Now to a certain extent I don't have a problem with this, however, between sitting down, ordering, and eating everything that was wrong with France, the French, the food, the drink, the restaurant. When the food came it was wrong, toppings didn't taste right, the toppings at their pizza hut where different, you get the picture. At one point they even glanced at me and talked about how the French managed to guzzle a full bottle of wine to themselves with every meal!!

This continued throughout the rest of the evening, and my embarrassment turned to amusement as I wondered why these people ever left Milton Keynes or Slough or wherever in the first place, but the icing was the restaurateur, hanging around and asking in loud French if everything was ok and making comments about how nice and well behaved the kids were, of course this set of ignorant idiots just nodded and continued muttering about this that and the other, oblivious to the fact that he understood every word they were saying. I had an absolute pocket of small change from my trip and after asking for the bill in French had managed to count it out to the last centime. After calling for the owner I just couldn't resist, in my bestest broadest Yorkshire, "Hope tha dunt mind me old cocker, but its all in shrap as I'm of t'home in t'mornin"
Keeping a straight face he replied "Nah mate thats fine, hope thas had a grand meal and have a safe trip"
Well the look on the families faces, red, they could have heated the place for a month. Anyway I laughed the entire way back to the tent and was still giggling when I fell into an exhausted slumber.

—

Day 20

Only another 52 hours until I have to be on a petrol station forecourt in Lourdes waiting for the bike bus to pick me up and return me to blighty, fortunately its only a couple of hours ride away with no hills, so plenty of options.

Overcast again but with the sun trying to breakout, the day started a little bit warmer at 15° convinced me it was worth staying around for the day and attempting to find the Cirque de Gavernie, a massive semi-circular amphitheatre of rock on the border with Spain.

What I should have done was left my tent and gear at the campsite, and either stayed there the night or risked having to pay for the night and gone to Anne's, but for some reason, unknown even to myself, I loaded all the gear onto the bike and set off on a circular route that would take in hundreds of metres of climbing, and so it was that I set off in the early morning light into Luz to find the coffee shop on the town square I had seen the previous afternoon.

I even had to wait for the bleeding coffee shop to open, I have never been able to lie in in a tent, being a postman doesn't help I suppose. The coffee shop in question was a coffee emporium, with more varieties and styles of coffee and pastries than the mind can take in. Each offering displayed frozen in time in whatever medium but leaving the customer in no doubt what they could expect. I was not disappointed after picking the largest fanciest looking of options, covered in a swirl of cream, topped with caramel and nuts, the glass was nearly a foot tall.

Once again the sun didn't disappoint and the temperature was soon climbing into the mid twenties. Until today my experiences with French roads and the drivers occupying them had been nothing but favourable, the surfaces had been remarkably smooth and pot-hole free apart from inside the odd town borders and the hardest part had been getting used to the Frenchman;s habit of pipping their horn to let you know they were about to pass. However on the road this morning heading towards the Spanish border the gloves were off. The Cirque must be on the itinerary of a multitude of tourist excursions and tours with coaches originating from all over Europe. This of course meant Britain also, and it was from a coach bearing a GB sticker and number plates that I had my first close call, the moron behind the wheel deciding that it was perfectly acceptable to pass me 10 yards from the apex of a hairpin corner on a road that was barely wider than he was. Another yard further on and I would have been forced over the cliff edge, as it was I came to a stop and managed to unclip before toppling over. The second close call came from the driver of a Spanish produce truck thinking that once he was past me then the entire thirty foot of his wagon must be also, this time forcing me off the side of the road and luckily onto a dirt verge that was only a short drop from the broken edge of the tarmac. Had this been my first day of riding in France I think I would have turned round and gone home!

The road off to the Cirque was surprisingly unmarked and it wasn't until I noticed that the volume of coach traffic had dropped to nought that I realised I must have started to ascend the climb over the top and towards the boarder with Spain. The road surface was nothing to write home about and the gradients had started to increase to well in excess of ten percent. Had I left all my gear in Luz I think I would possibly have continued to the boarder but the heat and extra effort of carrying the extra weight and the thought of the steep descent with canti brakes on such a poor road surface and I soon turned tail and headed back to find the road to the Cirque.

Turning off and dropping out of sight of the main road led to a massive car and coach park, with the road continuing the other side lined with tourist tat shops and food outlets, continuing on two wheels was a chore due to the volume of foot traffic. I did spot the coach that had nearly killed me earlier and did consider going over and offering a few words of advice to the driver but decided life was too short, and besides there were a lot of witnesses.!! The road to the actual amphitheatre soon turns into a track once the village runs out and tourists are left with the option of walking or taking a pony ride up, with the level of the crowds I did not feel safe locking the bike up with all my gear on and attempted to walk pushing the bike, it wasn't far though before I came across a rock formation that had to be traversed and meant having to turn round and abandon my visit. With hindsight I should have just locked the bike up and said sod it, but as it was I ended up trekking back to the town centre and choosing from one of the many cafes and restaurants for lunch. The duck and chips was very enjoyable and nearly worth the journey alone, for such a tourist place and with such a captive audience I was even pleasantly surprised by the price.

Fortunately the ride back down from the Cirque was uneventful and much easier than the way up as gravity made all the effort. Arriving back in Luz I thought I had better give Anne a quick ring to make sure she was still ok to host me that night, before starting the climb of the Tourmalet to Viella, the alternative would be a return to the campsite. Anne was busy when I rang and said it would be a couple of hours before she could break off and meet me to take me to her house, but if that was ok then she would meet me in the village square of Viella. Viella is a small mountain village on the lower slopes of the Tourmalet and consists of a cafe, a church and a stone market square with a notice board. The weather was slightly deteriorating toward low cloud when I arrived with a good hour to spare and unfortunately the cafe was closed. Anne arrived as advertised and led me half a street away to a small terraced house, garage and cellar on the ground floor and where I could store my bike. Anne and her partner where obviously keen cyclists, the area at the rear of the cellar housed a turbo trainer in front of a window looking out onto the steep slopes of the valley and a range of bikes propped against the walls, the most outstanding of these was a fat wheeled mountain bike, but not any mountain bike, a tandem mountain bike with full suspension!! The first time I had seen such a thing, I can't imagine tackling some of the trails I had seen guys on as an individual let alone on a tandem.

Anne only stayed long enough to show me to a bedroom and point out the bathroom before heading back to work, so after a quick shower I opted to get an hours kip before her return. When I woke up she was already home and cooking a meal, she apologised and said she had been hoping to take me to the village cafe that served excellent food and where she helped out in her spare time, unfortunately the chef/owner had fallen two days previously and broke his wrist and hence the reason why the place was closed. Anne did a great job of talking down her abilities in the kitchen but I can honestly say the food tasted marvellous and was as good as anything I had eaten the whole time I had been in France. Anne spoke English about as well as I speak French, enough to get by and be understood but not really enough to be conversational. I did gather that there was nothing to do in Viella with the cafe being shut and she was tired in any case having had to travel for work and would need to be up early the next day for the same reason. I also didn't fancy the slog back up from Luz had I gone out for the evening so I called it a night early on and retired to my bedroom to read until sleep came again.

Day 21

The early morning view through the roof window of mist hanging over the wooded slopes was one I could wake to every morning given the choice. The smell of moisture on fresh vegetation coupled with wood smoke reminded me of one of the things I was going to miss most when I returned home in a couple of days as well.

Anne was busy in the kitchen area when I walked in and again she apologised that breakfast would only be a drink and a biscuit but she was in a rush to get off and lock up and unless I wished to stay another night. With nothing to do other than climb the Tourmalet again I was happy to continue on my way, I had originally considered doing other climbs in the area if I had a spare day, but after the Cirque the day before the thought of having to climb fully loaded up the Col d'Aubisque didn't somehow float my boat. After 3 weeks of riding without having a complete day out of the saddle I was beginning to falter and lose a bit of enthusiasm, maybe it was the thought of another twenty-four hour coach journey the next day, or the thought of returning straight to work without a break that was doing it. With heartfelt thanks I left Viella with my pannier complete with half a homemade chocolate cake that was left from the evenings meal.

The weather was a little overcast with mist and low cloud hanging in the trees on the hillsides but with a promise of the sun to burn it all off later and indeed it had already started to brighten by the time I had descended into Luz, to give it further time to improve I stopped once again at the coffee emporium and with only an hour or so cycling in front of me I enjoyed a relaxed coffee before heading out of time in the opposite direction to yesterday . The contrast was like black and white, in this direction new tarmac had recently been laid (probably for the tour), and it was a steady downhill gradient with gentle sweeping corners. Once again the drivers were considerate and courteous and order seemed to have been restored to the world.

One thing that had cropped up in conversation with Anne the previous evening was the existence of a dedicated cycle path from a few kilometres outside of Luz, all the way into Lourdes, she said the entrance to it was a bit obscure and hard to find but with the help of a map I thought I had it located. Entering the town where it was supposed to start I recognised the industrial estate she had said was the easiest way to access it and after cycling through a firms car park, sure enough came across an obscure sign pointing in the direction of a cycle path. The cycle path was an old railway line that had been laid with glorious smooth tarmac. The campsite I had picked out near Argeles-Gazost actually bordered the cycle path but with some low cloud still around and for the aforementioned reasons I continued on to Lourdes and abandoned the idea of another climb, laden with gear or not.

As promised the cycle path continued most of the way into Lourdes through quiet and magnificent countryside before tapering out at the main road that my sat nav picked up as the road I should have been cycling in on, about a mile from the towns outskirts . I had not expected to stay in Lourdes for a night so I was relying on the sat nav to point me in the direction of a campsite, I thought it had failed me once again as it led me down what appeared to be a residential street, but sure enough behind a large hedge and through some ancient gates a driveway led to a quiet oasis complete with swimming pool. The sun was finally making an appearance and using the pool looked promising despite the morning's low cloud. Cycling to my designated spot, marked out with its own wooden stake, I overheard my new neighbours and discovered they where British. Unfortunately they were in the process of decamping but I discovered they were so late because the previous nights weather had been atrocious and they were hoping that the sun would have arrived earlier to dry out their gear. It wasn't until they had finally taken their tent down altogether that I realised they were just going to throw it away as their tour had come to an end and they didn't want the excess baggage. Drat I could have saved time and the risk of getting my own tent wet if I had just taken over theirs. As it was I asked if it would be ok to rescue it and take it home myself as it could be donated to my local scout troop that I had in the past been involved with and I had no worries over excess baggage. In conversation I also learned that Lourdes town centre was a good 30 minute walk away and to be prepared, they were unwilling to expand on that thought.

In the end after rescuing the tent I realised it was not worth rescuing, whilst up it had looked at a distance to be of decent quality but examining it close the material and weight pointed out that it was a very cheap affair that was only suitable for summer camping and festivals, basically after the two weeks use they had out of it, its only use now would be to cover my bike overnight and to replace my bent pegs and supply extra guy rope.

As it was still only lunchtime I decided to walk into Lourdes and find somewhere for a quick bite and explore the town. I had no idea what to expect, I knew it was a place people came to worship and it had great significance to the Catholic community. I am not a religious person myself and I really don't want to cause offence but..........

The first clue, even on the outskirts, was that it seemed every signpost also included the distance and direction you needed to travel to reach the grotto, the only other place I have come across this phenomenon is in Italy and Maranello, where every signpost points the way to Ferrari, I suppose in their own way they are both the holy grail. Walking into town I passed the ubiquitous Spa shop and decided the best plan was to buy the components of a picnic and head back to camp, have lunch a swim and get changed before walking the full distance into town and finding out what there was to see. I figured in a town of this size I would have no problem finding a decent place for an evening meal and making the most of my last night in France.

Setting off once again it was around 2pm when I reached the town centre, the town of Lourdes is large compared to everywhere else I had passed through in the preceding three weeks and was extremely busy with tourists and those on a pilgrimage to the famous grotto to try the holy water, it also had the first McDonalds I had seen this trip, read into that what you will. To me, Lourdes was a scary place, groups of teenagers wandering round dressed head to foot in nothing but white, shops selling nothing but white clothes, and shops selling nothing but religious icons and statues. Not one or two shops but twenty or thirty shops from the size of a corner shop up to a department store selling nothing but religious statues of biblical characters from the shepherds to Moses and the virgin Mary. These statues came in every size from an inch high to sit on your mantelpiece to three foot tall lined up in every window by their hundreds, I am sure there would be life sized available had I thought to ask.

The grotto itself is beautiful in its setting in magnificent gardens accessed through grand stone arches that adjoin the gold embossed entrance of the church were the faithful go to pray and ask forgive ness in their thousands. Even an agnostic like me who only attends church for weddings and funerals could not help be moved by the sight and atmosphere of this holy place, I had gone to visit not in search of anything in particular but with an open mind to accept whatever emotions and feelings presented themselves. Unfortunately it was spoiled more or less as soon as I passed under one of the arches and started to move towards the grotto itself. Whilst not exactly a theme park it was like one. Those wishing to enter the grotto are presented with a queuing system reminiscent of a popular ride with signs stating the expected waiting time. The faithful light candles for loved ones and these are mounted on spikes outside the grotto in partially open sided green house like structures that spread along the edge of the walkways radiating a fantastic amount of heat, more reminiscent I would have thought of hell. Candles are available to buy from conveniently located kiosks and vending machines. Vending machines dotted every few yards also vend small vials of holy water and miniature bibles. Other machines vend containers of various sizes that can be filled with holy water by the purchaser. Queues form at various standpipes that dispense the holy and healing waters of Lourdes with people filling everything from the 1oz glass keepsakes to 20 gallon containers on wheels, a donation is kindly accepted.

Walking the length of the gardens brings you to a lawn with crosses of all descriptions and sizes planted by pilgrims that have carried them from all over the world, on the whole a moving experience, and for the devoted I am sure it is a lifetimes ambition, but one in my opinion looking from the outside as it were, that had been at the very best tainted by the ugly face of commercialism. I was glad I had visited, I just felt sad that what could or should have been a more moving/ private experience had been ruined, it would have been interesting to talk to others with a more defined purpose to find out their views.

Foregoing the delights of McDonald's I had turned my nose up at all the various eateries on my path back to the campsite and once again found myself with the option of pizza or nothing, so my final meal in France was going to be pizza, its a good job I like pizza, France was beginning to remind me of the old Monty Python sketch, just substitute Pizza for Spam and there you have it.

Day 22

The coach left from a petrol station on the main road out of Lourdes at eleven in the morning, the departure point was a five minute ride from the campsite straight down the road. With no particular desire to return into Lourdes I instead opted to have a lie in and set off at around ten am, I had noticed a large supermarket on the opposite side of the carriageway to the service station and even had that been closed (it being Sunday) I figured that the service station itself would at least sell coffee and pastries.

As it happened the supermarket did open on a Sunday but not until after the time I would risk missing the coach had it arrived even a few minutes early, I had just cycled back from investigating the supermarket opening times when I received a text from the coach to say that they were running over an hour behind schedule. Oh well back on the bike and around the loop back to wait for the supermarket to open its doors, at least the weather was pleasant enough for hanging about.

Stocked up on fruit juice, a 10 pack of stubbies, chocolate and pre-packed sandwiches, I was struggling to get everything loaded into the panniers and ended up pushing the bike across the dual carriageway whilst carrying a bag of shopping as opposed to riding down to the roundabout and back up the other side. In the time I had spent waiting and shopping a couple of other passengers had arrived waiting for the coach. As it was now getting warmer and the coach had announced it was as going to be even later it only seemed natural to open up a couple of stubbies and swap war stories from our adventures. Whether the others thought I was an alcoholic passing round the bears before lunch on a Sunday stood in a petrol station car park I have no idea, regardless they didn't refuse! My abiding memory of the wait for the coach was a great chap called Nigel who had been riding around Pau, I think he should have been offered the job of chief of Pau tourism such was his evangelistic ramblings about the place, he had liked it so much he had decided he was selling up and moving out there as soon as the opportunity arose.

Eventually the coach arrived and after loading the gear and bike all there was to do was sit back and look forward to the next rest stop as the 24 hour journey stretched out in front.

Day 23

The overnight ferry journey was at least sparsely populated and after enjoying a warm meal with Nigel (as much as one can enjoy cuisine on a ferry) I managed to get a few minutes of comfort stretched across a nicely padded bench seat.

2012 was the year of the London Olympics and as the coach headed onto the M25 around London in dawns early light the weirdest most extraordinary sight of my trip was about to present itself. Cycling along the inside lane was a group of eight cyclists with the rear man flying the flag of china on a long pole fastened to a rear pannier, no doubt a trip to remember for them as well.

Finally Wakefield was the next stop and despite having rung the wife to let her know of my imminent arrival thirty minutes earlier, it was still another half hour before she turned up, maybe I should have just biked the few miles home!

Epilogue

In the months that followed more or less all the monies pledged by generous and kind people up and down the country where received by SOL and in total I believe over three thousand pounds was donated to help with emergency kennelling costs.

Sighthounds OnLine (SOL) after helping countless number of hounds in kennels around the world effectively disbanded twelve months later. Their main fundraising activity had been through online auctions that relied on the charity of companies and individuals donating goods to auction. Seeing the success of SOL led to other similar organisations develop, started with the best of intentions but diluting the charity pot. Over the many years that SOL operated more and more individual hound rescues also copied SOL's fundraising template and this led to several auctions running at the same time on several websites and individual bulletin boards. Unfortunately the easiest way for these charities to try and gain gifts to auction was to approach those that were regular contributers to SOL and eventually the burden was getting too much. With a lack of income stream and many of the charities SOL was raising money for now raising money for themselves through the internet medium the officers of SOL made the decision that the money they were having to spend on keeping the website alive would be better used keeping hounds alive and moved on, with at least one of them, the lovely Wendy, sinking her life savings into starting "Kim's home for elderly/abused dogs".

This short narration of my adventures in aid of SOL was originally meant to boost the SOL emergency kennel fund, with its demise any royalties I receive will be used to continue to provide for foster hounds in my care and Greyhound charities around the country.

HANK 'The Hank Man' ???? - 2013 Fostered from Bristol Dawg

'Born to Run'

Five years at the peak of your game, the black messiah,
Chasing the mechanical hare you never did tire
A thousand corners always in the lead
The greatest greyhound, the punters number one seed.
Living fast on bright lights, applause and accolade,
It wasn't your choice the speed started to fade.

No more the fastest, the darling of the crowd,
Fourth and fifth your fickle owner not so proud
After a life with a kings ransom staked at ever race
Now left alone in unheated kennel looking for a home space
Surely not to have to wait for long
Not you, the one time subject of the punters song.

Time passed so swiftly where did it go
With each prospective family looking in and saying no.
Brindles, whites, fawns, out of the kennels flew
But even a champion no home offers for a black dog like you
Time was cruel as was the mistress fate
Arthritis, corns and no teeth left from the slop you ate.

Another winter, cold snow, wind, darkness and rain
Ten years of living, ready to curl up and succumb finally to the pain.
WAKE UP shouts Gold, your cell mate, we'll make a run, a jail break.
Just as Bristol DAWG show up, Elkie shakes her head, for Pity"s sake.
I know a pair of homes for dogs like you
Through SOL website, a warm bed after all you've been through.

The day dawned at last to move from kennels to the warmth you seek
As you traveled North the weather turned from bad to bleak
Snow flurries turned into a storm with inches settling on the ground
You gazed out and cried please don't make us turn round.
At last the pair of you ended up on my fire side
Gold to wait for clear roads and his onward ride.

Your new companions and a home to explore
Warmth, cuddles, food, treats, beds and more
Holidays, walks, fun, laughter, despite suffering and pain

Never a growl, a mutter, no matter what, did you complain
For three years you brought loving and great joy
Now with tears and heavy heart, I say so long Hank, my silly big black boy

DINO 1998 - 2009 Adopted ex TIA

'Born to Flapp'

Bred to grace the flapping track but with heart murmer and lame of leg,
Soon to be rejected, abandoned to steal and beg.
Avoiding cars, lorries and starvation,
TIA greyhound rescue was your salvation.

But by now an unsociable fella with all trust lost,
How on earth could they justify the cost?
When you attacked any kennel mate,
And showed no interest in the hand from which you ate.

Looking for a blue bitch to adopt I came,
He's a black dog they said, so pretty much the same.
So like a sucker I agreed and even paid,
For the first few weeks a mistake I thought we'd made.

You would lie upon your bed and give the cold shoulder,
Until you knew you were staying then you got bolder.
Kicking us from the sofa and then our bed,
Finally using our laps to lay your head.

Well old boy after nine fantastic years,
The time as come for me to shed some tears.
As I lay you down to rest,
I know at the bridge you will show Mick the Miler who is best.

Farewell my best friend.

Printed in Great Britain
by Amazon